A LIFELONG JOURNEY:

STAYING WELL WITH MANIC DEPRESSION/BIPOLAR DISORDER

A LIFELONG JOURNEY:

STAYING WELL WITH MANIC DEPRESSION/BIPOLAR DISORDER

Sarah Russell

MICHELLE ANDERSON PUBLISHING
MELBOURNE

First published 2005 by
Michelle Anderson Publishing Pty Ltd
PO Box 6032 Chapel Street North
South Yarra 3141
Tel: 03 9826 9028
Fax: 03 9826 8552
Email: mapubl@bigpond.net.au
website: www.michelleandersonpublishing.com

Reprinted 2005

Cover design: Deb Snibson, Modern Art Production Group
Typeset in Australia by Midland Typesetters
Printed in Australia by Griffin Press

National Library of Austrralia cataloguing-in-publication data

Russell, Sarah, 1961–.
A lifelong journey: staying well with manic
depression/bipolar mood disorder.
ISBN 085572 357 2

1. Manic-depressive illness. 2. Manic-depressive illness –
Anecdotes. I. Title.

616.895

CONTENTS

This book is dedicated to Jack Cade, and his dad, John

ACKNOWLEDGMENTS

The idea for this book developed during dog walks and dinner conversations with colleagues and friends. Margie Nunn, Jan Browne, Clare Carberry, Philomena Horsely, Marilys Guillemin, Carol Harvey, Ellie Fossey, Merinda Epstein, and Yoland Wadsworth each brought something special to the dining table.

The preliminary research was funded by beyondblue Victorian centre of excellence in depression and related disorders grants program. During this research, people from all around Australia accepted an invitation to share how they lived well with manic depression. Their collective wisdom provided the inspiration for this book. I offer my sincere thanks to all who gave permission for me to re-tell parts of their story in this book. I also offer my thanks to those who provided feedback on early drafts of the book. In particular, I thank Gillian Wilson and Neil Cole.

As always, I am thankful to Joan Russell, Jack Cade and Jan Browne for their unfailing support, encouragement, patience and, of course, proof-reading.

INTRODUCTION

STAYING WELL WITH A MENTAL ILLNESS

We read so much about the bleak side of mental illness. We hear about the high rates of suicide, substance abuse, divorce, unemployment, and criminal behaviour. We hear much less about all of us who stay well.

Many of us with manic depression, also known as bipolar disorder, are living happy and fulfilling lives. We may have our ups and downs, but many people living with manic depression are able to hold down jobs and certainly manage to stay out of prison.

This book describes how people with manic depression manage to stay well. People who contributed to this collection are working as builders, social workers, engineers, lawyers, stock brokers, nurses, general practitioners, factory workers and so on. Many are parents. After all, manic-depression is an episodic illness: most of us, most of the time, are able to enjoy our lives.

This book brings diverse voices together. Each chapter contains personal stories. These stories are based on contributors' experiences of living with manic depression. For personal reasons, most contributors prefer to be identified with a pseudonym. To further respect their privacy, certain details of stories have been changed. However, the essence of each contributor's experience remains the same.

Each story speaks about manic depression in a personal and unique way. Some stories contribute similar information about staying well. In this way, the stories support and validate each other. They provide evidence that people with manic depression can, and do, stay well.

This book also includes information from the professional literature. Rather than dominate the stories, the professional voice merely provides another perspective. Unfortunately, the professional perspective focuses on people with manic depression when they are unwell. The focus on 'patients', 'clients' and 'consumers' often blinds health care professionals to 'people' with manic depression who stay well.

Manic depression is often portrayed as a 'nightmare'. However, this has not been my experience of the illness. The illness, particularly the manic component which provides the energy (and the desire!) to clean the house (among other things) at 3 am, can be quite amazing. What can be a 'nightmare', however, is other people's response to the illness. It is common for friends to send 'Get Well Soon' cards to sufferers of physical illnesses. Such compassion is less evident during episodes of mental illness. In fact, people often choose to keep episodes of mental illness shrouded in silence and secrecy.

To be with a person who is experiencing an episode of manic depression can be exhausting, even terrifying. To acknowledge the impact that this illness has on my friends, I say: *'I do not suffer from manic-depression – my friends suffer from my manic-depression'.* During an episode of depression, I simply sat silently and stared. It was a catatonic, psychotic depression. I have no memory of this, but my friends and family do. During an episode of mania, on the other hand, I neither sat still nor quietly. My mind and mouth were in overdrive. I said whatever ideas were on my mind without any consideration for the consequences.

Like others who suffer chronic illnesses, my challenge has been to control the symptoms so that they do not interfere with my life. With insight, education, experience and time, I learnt to manage the illness as a person with diabetes must learn to manage her sugar levels. I learnt to stay well.

Not surprisingly, the things that help to keep me well are the same things that help all people to stay well. I benefit from eating healthy foods, exercising, sleeping well, laughing and so on. We all do. However, with manic depression, I also need to make specific changes to my lifestyle to stay well. With kindness, support and trust of close friends, including my mother, I developed my own 'Stay Well Plan'. My stay well plan includes a daily dose of lithium. Equally important are my work, friends, Mt Martha beach, and, of course, sleep.

A few years ago, I discovered that a colleague also experienced manic depression. I was surprised to find that we relied on different ways to prevent relapses of illness. It sparked my curiosity to explore other people's experiences of staying well. People from many different walks of life contributed their story of living with manic depression. These stories confirm that staying well is rarely just about seeing a psychiatrist and taking prescribed medication. It is often about so much more.

Contributors to this book describe interesting and varied ways to stay well. They learnt (often through trial and error) what worked for them, and what did not work. Many gained expertise in managing their manic depression from their own life experiences, including experiences of illness. Their stories show the value of life experience in learning how to stay well.

People with manic depression describe episodes of manic depression as traumatic and disruptive. Episodes of illness were often one of the most distressing things to happen in their lives. This distress is due, in part, to the illness itself. It is also due to inadequacies within the mental health system and negative community attitudes. After experiencing the humiliation that so often accompanies treatment for mental illness, contributors to this book describe doing everything within their power to avoid another episode of illness. They found ways to stay well.

Contributors describe their journey with manic depression as a lifelong one. During the journey, they learn to become mindful of their illness. This mindfulness helps them to stay well. For many, the beginning of the journey was the most difficult period. In the early days, they experienced periods of unwellness, misdiagnosis, disbelief and anger. It took time, sometimes a long time, to accept the diagnosis.

People with manic depression describe acceptance as a key to being able to live well. Acceptance gave them the strength to navigate their journey with manic depression. The next step was acquiring knowledge about manic depression, and then developing strategies to stay well. These strategies gave them courage to take control of their illness and get on with living.

This book describes many different journeys with manic depression. Chapter one begins by describing the illness and defining some of the medical jargon. When people are first diagnosed, medical information and advice can be overwhelming. There is often too much information, too fast. For some, however, there was no information. Instead, they began their journey with manic depression undiagnosed and untreated. The second chapter contains stories of unnecessary and time-consuming detours when people were not diagnosed correctly. Once people received the correct diagnosis, the next stage of the journey was finding a suitable therapist and accessing information about manic depression. This was easier for some than others.

In chapters three and four, people with manic depression reveal a range of therapies they use to stay well. It is often a matter of finding what works best for each individual person. Most contributors take lithium, though other medications work better for some people. They describe medication as merely one of many therapies that are used to stay well. Most contributors describe the importance of getting enough sleep. Other popular therapies include diet, exercise, yoga, meditation, and cognitive behavioral therapy.

In chapter five, people with manic depression describe the importance of kindness and compassion from their support networks. This kindness did not just come from family members. It also came from friends, lovers, colleagues, pets, churches, community groups, mental health organisations and health care professionals.

Chapter six brings together a wealth of knowledge and experience of staying well with manic depression. It also contains some examples of 'Stay Well Plans'. Many contributors to this book have stayed well for over ten years, some for much longer. They have much wisdom to share.

Chapter 1

What is manic depression?

Manic depression is an episodic mental illness. It is marked by changes in mood, thought, energy and behaviour. Behaviour can be hyperactive, expansive and seductive, or it can be reclusive, sluggish, and suicidal.[1] Manic depression can be treated, but not cured. Having an incurable, chronic illness is a frightening prospect – until you realise that you can control it and learn to manage the symptoms.

Many contributors describe living with manic depression as a lifelong learning process. The book begins with Jodie. Her journey with manic depression had a troubled beginning and many set backs. Her story compares uncontrolled and controlled manic depression. It shows the social, emotional and financial costs of uncontrolled manic depression. It also demonstrates the impact of negative social attitudes. In order to live a better life with manic depression, Jodie made significant changes to her life. She is not afraid of the illness any more. She is able to control manic depression and stay well.

> I am a 29 year old, single woman with no children. I was diagnosed with manic depression (this is my preference for naming the illness) ten years ago. One of

the best things I can say about my illness now is that I am not scared of it anymore. I believe that I have the power to control it. I have learnt how to manage my symptoms.

Three years ago, I began counselling for a reason other than manic depression. I have been seeing the counsellor on a weekly basis ever since then. This counselling has been my saving grace. Prior to counselling, I was in hospital more times than I can count. I have received numerous treatments with electroconvulsive therapies (ECTs) and prescribed nearly every antidepressant under the sun.

It was only last week that my counsellor told me I was, without a doubt, a 'total success story'. As you can imagine, this 'success story' is a result of many very difficult times and choices, many home truths being ingrained, frustration, relapses, learning to set limits and boundaries, developing insight into my illness and the things that set me off, safety nets, and harm minimisation strategies.

It has been three years now without an episode, and I am generally stable with minor blips. This seems to be a miracle as I thought I was doomed to be chronically ill for the rest of my life. I have finally reached the stage where I, my family, psychologist and psychiatrist are fairly certain that if I keep doing what I'm doing, I will never go back into hospital or become significantly ill again.

Changes I have made to stay well include moving from a 'party house' in the city (which I thrived on) to living by myself on the Mornington Peninsula, close to the ocean. I left a very highly paid, stressful and 'social' job as an events manager in the city. I am now a full-time student, finishing my Certificate IV Community Services. I also gave up smoking marijuana and moved away from people who were not good for me.

I have learnt to take my pills without resentment – I take the pills in one gulp to get it over and done with quickly. I have finally realised that I can not do everything, so I limit my social activities and my involvement in other projects. I have also established regular sleeping times and other routines. This helps me to manage the illness.

I now have the capability and insight to see episodes coming on. Early signs usually include talking very quickly and doing one hundred things at once. I feel a sense of boredom which makes me crave some excitement. So I begin to binge drink and behave impulsively, including unsafe sexual behaviour.

My intention is never to go to hospital again. So when I see or feel these warning signs, I have my own action plan. My action plan has been constantly revised and updated throughout my illness, particularly during the last three years. This action plan prevents me from sliding further. From the day I was diagnosed, I have disclosed my illness to friends and family. I have been able to develop my action plan in conjunction with them. I am extremely lucky to have fantastic and supportive family and friends who understand my need to cancel sometimes, to have quiet times.

Ultimately I would like to work in the mental health field – with young people. When I was young and first diagnosed, I refused to accept my illness and refused to take medication. I was involved in many dangerous activities and caused a great deal of stress to my family. I also lost many friends as a result of my illness and my behaviour. I would therefore like to help young people to deal with the illness better than I did. If you learn about the illness, and accept it, you have a better chance of managing it.

I am dismayed by the attitudes of some teachers at school. They even tell jokes about 'manic depressives'. I am also utterly astounded, and I must say angry, at some marketing ploys I have seen to make mental illness 'sexy'. There is a company which has three self tanning products on the market – 'Bipolar', 'Schizophrenic' and 'Neurotic'.

The majority of the people I have been in contact with over the period of my illness generally believe that manic depression is the same as schizophrenia. They believe there is no hope for recovery or stable periods. Most believe that people with manic depression are 'crazy'. There is no real understanding about what manic depression is. I am very interested in the portrayal of people with manic depression by the media. There is a character on a TV show (Stingers) who has manic depression. He will be receiving ECT on this week's episode.

Authentic accounts of people living with manic depression are found in real life, not in the movies. Unfortunately, movies perpetuate only extreme stereotypes – people with manic depression are often portrayed as violent, frightening, suicidal, ridiculous, or even as 'mad geniuses'. In the movies, people with manic depression are rarely portrayed as just ordinary people with a manageable illness.

Manic depression is a mood disorder. The illness is characterised by episodes of mania (or hypomania), depression and mixed states of manic and depressed symptoms. *Mania* is defined by health care professionals as an abnormally elevated, expansive or irritable mood with brief psychotic periods. *Hypomania* is an abnormally elevated mood without psychotic periods. It is a milder form of mania. *Depression* is a feeling of melancholy, hopelessness and dejection. Depression impacts on emotions, thinking, behaviour and physical well being. *Cyclothymia* is the cycling of hypomanic episodes with depression. *Mixed states* are when both manic/hypomanic symptoms and depressive symptoms occur at the same time (e.g. depression with racing thoughts).

Health care professionals currently sub-divide the illness into bipolar disorder 1 and 2. Bipolar 1 is characterised by manic episodes that are often followed by episodes of depression. Bipolar 2 disorder is characterised by major depressive episodes alternating with episodes of hypomania (not mania).[2] The distinction between bipolar I disorder and bipolar 2 disorder hinges on the boundary between mania and hypomania.[3]

Criteria for diagnosis

Some health care professionals believe it is preferable to use a broad spectrum to diagnose manic depression/bipolar disorder. However, the Diagnostic and Statistical Manual of Mental Disorders (DSM-IV) has narrow criteria. For example, according to the DSM-IV, mania lasts at least one week while hypomania lasts at least four days.[4]

Symptoms of mania

During an episode of mania, people often experience a decreased need for sleep. It is common for people to wake up feeling energetic after only a few hours of sleep. Sometimes, people do not sleep at all. Instead, they stay awake all night with ideas entering their mind at a rapid rate. Health care professionals refer to this as 'flight of ideas'. People may also become obsessed with a particular issue, topic or event. On the other hand, they may be easily distracted with their attention drawn to unimportant or irrelevant external stimuli.

With so much energy, and so many new ideas, it is not surprising that people experiencing an episode of mania feel the need to communicate – talk, write, phone, SMS, email – with a sense of urgency and importance. Health care professionals describe this as 'pressure of speech' and note that it may be socially inappropriate to be so outspoken.[5]

During an episode of mania, people may experience themselves as being more capable and competent than normal. This is sometimes referred to as 'delusions of grandeur'. According to health care professionals, the inflated self-esteem is out of proportion to reality and, again, may be socially embarrassing.[6] In addition to feeling embarrassed, delusions of grandeur may encourage excessive shopping sprees, sexual indiscretions, or foolish business investments. This risky behaviour may have serious long-term consequences.

Symptoms of depression

There are a number of symptoms associated with depression. These symptoms include significant changes in appetite and weight – some people experience a decrease in appetite (and weight), others an increase. There are also changes in sleep patterns, either insomnia or excessive sleep. People become very tired both physically (loss of energy) and mentally (diminished ability to concentrate). People may experience feelings of worthlessness, or excessive guilt. Some may have recurrent thoughts of death.

For people to be diagnosed with a major depression, they must experience either depressed mood or loss of interest/ pleasure in activities. According to health care professionals, depressed mood is indicated by either subjective report (e.g. a person feels sad or empty) or observation made by others (e.g. person appears tearful).[7]

Ellen finds the diagnostic language obscure. She finds it difficult to understand exactly what 'inappropriate', 'excessive' or 'diminished' mean. She also wonders how 'socially embarrassing' is gauged, and by whom. When she was first diagnosed, her psychiatrist used terms such as 'flight of ideas' and 'pressure of speech' without explaining what these terms meant. This made it difficult for her to manage the symptoms of her illness.

> When I was told that I had bipolar disorder, the doctor's explanation was hopelessly inadequate. He simply said 'think yourself lucky you don't have schizophrenia'. I did not have a clue what he was talking about.
>
> I've had the illness for years. But I still do not recognise when I am about to go high. I do not have the slightest notion what is happening to me. The psychiatrist explained that I needed to be aware when I get 'speech pressure' and 'flighty ideas'. It is hard for me to recognise these symptoms when I do not understand what the terminology means. What does it feel like to have a 'flighty idea'?
>
> For many years, I did not realise that manic depression and bipolar disorder were the same illness. I have

since learnt that there are a range of different names for this illness: 'bipolar disorder', 'bipolar mood disorder', 'bipolar affective disorder' and 'manic depression'. This is all very confusing. I prefer 'bipolar disorder'. 'Bipolar affective disorder' is unfortunately abbreviated to BAD and 'manic depression' gives others the impression that we are all 'maniacs'. I really do not like it when people call it manic depression.

Some brochures provide a check list of the different symptoms for mania and depression. They use words such as 'inappropriate', 'excessive' or 'diminished', but I am never sure what this means. I doubt many of us need a check list to recognise when we feel depressed. I realise I am depressed when I can't get out of bed in the morning. If this continues for a few days, I call my psychiatrist and tell him that I am about to take extra anti-depressants – he knows that I am sensible about pills. I also make myself go out. When I feel depressed, staying home alone makes things worse.

I find mania much harder to pick. These brochures list the symptoms of mania as elevated mood, increased energy, over activity, rapid thinking/talking, lack of inhibitions, grandiose plans and reduced need for sleep. I would be pretty far gone if I had all these symptoms. To manage this illness, I need to intervene a long time before I start making grandiose plans and taking myself on a major shopping spree.

Although brochures helped me to understand bipolar disorder a bit better, they did not help me to recognise my early warning signs. This is something I had to learn with the help of my friends. Fortunately, I have some close friends who know me well. They live

> nearby and are able to easily recognise when I am getting high. They assure me that I have never been 'socially embarrassing' – whatever that means. I normally just get stuck on an idea and start to talk quickly about things that are suddenly terribly important to me. I have asked these few friends to tell me if they think I am getting a bit high. If I don't listen to them, they have my permission to phone my psychiatrist.
>
> For years, I have tried to manage this illness on my own, but I do not have any insight when I am high. So to prevent a relapse, I take my medication every day. I now recognise that I can't stay well without medication. I have tried, believe me. Like most people I dislike having to rely on pills. I fought against taking it but I have learnt bipolar is caused by a chemical imbalance. So first and foremost I take the medication. But even with medication, I have mood swings.
>
> Talking about my illness with people who do not understand only makes things worse. So I no longer confide in my family who have no insight into bipolar. The people who monitor my moods are people who understand my illness. I trust my friends completely. If they say I am manic, I am!

People with manic depression often learn to manage their illness with the assistance of specific people. These people may be friends, not family members. It may not always be appropriate for health care professionals to discuss diagnosis and treatment with family members. Sometimes, it may be more appropriate for health care professionals to consult with a lover, friend, colleague or neighbour than a family member.

When health care professionals consult appropriately, and take a comprehensive history, people with manic depression are more likely to be correctly diagnosed. However, there is no objective test to confirm the diagnosis. Instead, health care professionals rely on their clinical judgment to distinguish between the symptoms of manic depression and other illnesses and conditions.

When Grace began spending more money than she could afford, her husband assumed it was the 'change of life'. However, her doctor immediately diagnosed manic depression, not menopause. She has taken lithium ever since. However, some controversy surrounds the diagnosis and treatment of psychiatric illness during menopause.[8]

I'm 83. I became unwell during menopause, thirty five years ago. It was hard on my husband – I spent a lot of money when we couldn't afford it. He got me to see a doctor who immediately diagnosed manic depression. It was a bit of a shock because my husband and three children all thought it was just the change of life.

I've taken the lithium for thirty-five years. I see my local doctor for my blood pressure. He also gives me the tablets for the manic depression, but we never discuss my moods or mental state. I read somewhere that I was meant to have blood tests, so I asked my GP. He phoned some specialist and I have been having tests ever since. No-one ever tells me the results, so I assume that they are OK.

Years ago, I told a few friends about being diagnosed with manic depression. But I don't talk about it much now. There doesn't seem to be any point. I'm happy, and I've lived a normal life. I had the illness. But

I don't have it any more. To be honest, I'm not sure that I ever did. It may well have just been the change of life.

For many years, women with manic depression have noticed a link between episodes of illness and their hormone levels. At certain times of the month, women are often more aware of extreme mood swings. In the absence of an objective test to monitor manic depression, Jamie listens to what her body and mind is telling her.

Unfortunately there is no objective measure for monitoring the severity of mental illness. There is no blood test, CT scan or thermometer to quantify the discomfort. Externally I can look 100% and feel 3% inside. No plaster or splints on the outside, no interesting and acceptable story to share with our friends about an accident and/or an operation we required.

It is not only people external to ourselves who underestimate the extent of the disorder. For many years, I did not make any allowances for the fact that I had bipolar disorder. This was partly because I was fortunate. Once on the right combination of medication, I was symptom free. I therefore expected my body to work and play as hard as all my friends and colleagues with full health. I had to learn the hard way, that 'symptom free' is not equivalent to being as resilient as the people around me who do not have bipolar disorder.

I am a registered nurse. I discovered that I loved the autonomy and responsibility of critical care nursing and undertook qualifications in this area. Obviously, not everyone is suited to this type of work. It is often emotionally stressful and confronting work. It also involves frequent night duty rotations. I used to think that I must be able to do this – I should be able to do this – because everyone around me can. Once trained in the area, it seemed foolish to walk away from a good income. I can now see that I was punishing myself by continuing to work in this area once I sensed the strain involved. I was not making any allowances for the fact that I had bipolar disorder, particularly the fact that I may be more sensitive to this environment than others around me.

Kay Jamison's book,[9] while highly valuable and insightful, was double-edged for someone with my temperament. On one hand, I gained a great deal of reassurance from the idea that you could have gruelling manic and depressive episodes and be a professor of psychiatry (and 'come out' about it). On the other hand, this idea also instilled in me an assumption that I should be able to 'at least' attain and sustain a career in critical care nursing.

My illness is invisible. How would I know whether everyone else was facing up to an equivalent challenge, silently and invisibly? The stigma of mental illness ensures a silence over such topics. Many people are experiencing this mental illness in more difficult social and financial circumstances than mine and are living amazing lives. But the fact is that the great majority of the friends and colleagues that I expected myself to measure up to did not face an equivalent challenge. I could have been easier on myself a lot earlier. Also, the nursing profession did not acknowledge that working in this area is often stressful and confronting. Minimal opportunities for debriefing were made available, and 'supervision' is a concept I have only discovered since working in my new job.

Now, finally, I listen to what my body is 'telling me'. I know myself. It has taken practice and patience to recognise when I need to push myself a bit – to exercise or to be with people – and when I should rest and replenish. I respect my limitations. I know my strengths. I compare myself with myself, not with others who have different challenges and attributes to mine.

An analogy is a teenager with fair skin that lies on silver reflective tanning sheets until she is red and sore in a vain attempt to develop a suntan. Summer after summer she pursues the unachievable and suffers the painful consequences. Then, one day, she accepts that she has fair skin. She accepts that others are born with more melanin, with naturally olive skin – that these people can tolerate hours in the sun which she cannot. And thanks to community education about the danger of skin cancer and how to be 'sun smart' the fair teenager now feels good about applying sunscreen, wearing a t-shirt and a hat, and even appreciates the warning signs that her skin gives – that encourages her to leave the sun earlier than those around her.

I believe mental health organisations are invaluable in promoting much needed community education about mental illness, in order to end the stigma and the silence and the unnecessary anguish still associated with mental illness today. Maybe one day these organisations will succeed in making treatment for mental illness as acceptable, and as well understood by the community, as the 'slip-slop-slap' campaign.

This story shows how people with manic depression move beyond professional criteria and develop their own criteria for everyday life. To stay well, Jamie is mindful of manic depression even when she is symptom free. This mindfulness involves accepting her personal strengths and limitations. In making decisions about her life, she takes into account the fact that she has a chronic illness. This awareness enables her to live well and prevent further episodes of illness.

A medical diagnosis, not a label

In the early 1980s, the American Psychiatric Association replaced the term 'manic depression' with 'bipolar disorder'. Some people prefer to continue with the old name because it describes the way moods alternate between the extremes of mania and depression. Others believe 'manic depression' conjures up an image of maniacs. They hope that changing the name to 'bipolar disorder' will help to change community attitudes towards the illness.

Community attitudes are largely influenced by the way a diagnosis is applied. For example, when people are described as 'manic depressive', 'bipolar', 'diabetic' or 'asthmatic', the medical diagnosis becomes a label that defines the whole person, not just the illness. Yet, it is the illness that is the problem, not the person. This distinction is clear to Robert. As a general practitioner, he shares his personal and professional experiences.

I'm a 54 year old general practitioner. My strategy is to see the problem as the manic depression and not me as a person. I separate myself from the illness. I see the need for me to be in control of the manic depression, so that it doesn't influence my life too much.

Unfortunately, I sometimes need to take high doses of steroids for a physical illness. This has resulted in several episodes of both mania and depression. So, in some ways, my strategy for avoiding manic depression is to avoid high dose steroids. However, this is not always possible.

When I think about community attitudes to mental illness, I often think of the asthma campaign. When I started out as a GP in the 1970s, we often avoided using the term asthma and substituted 'wheezy bronchitis' so as to not scare the parents. With better outcomes, we called it asthma again. Then Geoff Marsh became vice captain of the Australian cricket team, despite having asthma. This helped to change community attitudes towards asthma.

I have spent much of my time working in psychiatry. Every Mental Health Week the public would be fed more horror stories. They would be told just how bad these illnesses were. The public learnt nothing except that there was no point in funding mental health because it was a waste of time. Where were the success stories?

Rather than highlight the downside of illnesses, I focus on what people achieve despite the problem. There are plenty of people getting on with their lives in a successful and productive way despite their illness. If that should be the normal outcome in the public's perception then they would be far less likely to deny funding for rehabilitation, getting back to work programs and so on.

The outcomes for mental illness are so much better in developing countries. I often look there to get an idea of what should be a reasonable expectation of outcome. When I was living in Mozambique there was this guy who used to come to our back door to sell us veggies. Despite our difficulties with communication, this man seemed a bit all over the place. Eventually, he stopped coming round and I forgot about him. Some time later I was asked to give a talk at the local school. This man was the class teacher. Apparently, every now and again, he would become unwell and go off for a while. When he was well again, he would return. Obviously, having no welfare system he would have to organise an income even when unwell. This need to keep doing some work, and to continue social interaction with the community, is thought to be one of the reasons for the better outcomes in these countries.

Manic depression is an episodic illness that can affect us all. It is found among all ages, races, ethnic groups, social classes and professional groups. It affects 1–2% of people, with men and women being equally affected. The illness tends to run in families – it seems quite likely that manic depression has a genetic link, though social factors may also contribute.

There is an enormous spectrum in the way people experience the symptoms of manic depression. Some people experience severe episodes of both mania and depression throughout their entire lives; others experience less severe symptoms less often. In addition, people respond differently to treatment. Despite these differences, the illness trajectory can be influenced by stay well strategies. With knowledge, experience and time, many people with manic depression learn to control their symptoms and prevent relapses.

Speaking the unspeakable

With the Australian population being around 20 million people, there are at least 200,000 accounts of people living with manic depression. It is likely that most Australians have encountered people with manic depression, though often unknowingly. In day-to-day contexts – at work, on public transport, at the local football club – manic depression is present-yet-absent. The person with manic depression is mindful that the illness is present, but others may not be.

People who stay well with manic depression are often reluctant to talk about their illness. So, instead of hearing stories about people with manic depression who stay well, we predominantly hear about extreme behaviour when people with manic depression are unwell. These negative stories reinforce the perception that people with manic depression are destined to a life of madness and suffering.

Like many others, Emily only heard negative accounts of manic depression. She had the impression that it was not possible to stay well with manic depression. For the first twelve years of her journey with manic depression, Emily experienced fear and uncertainty about what her life was going to be like – she felt sure that her future was hopeless. Without any role models, it was a long, hard road to where she is today.

I'm 43 years old. I began to be seriously affected by manic depression around age 19, when I was an arts/law student. I went through twelve or so particularly difficult years. During acute phases of illness I was in and out of hospitals, both private and public, before gradually regaining equilibrium. During this difficult time, it would have been helpful to know that others had learnt to manage this illness. I did not know anyone. Back then, I could not even find out about anyone who had gone through an illness as disruptive as mine and come out 'OK'. Occasionally I heard about the odd famous figure of the distant past, such as Nebuchadnezzar. But this did not give me much hope.

I finished off my arts degree at Melbourne University and have been working in publishing positions for the past five years. It is still far from easygoing or bed-of-roses stuff. However, my problems have definitely moved into the domain where lots of other people have many of the same issues to deal with, day-to-day.

The silence around manic depression is slowly changing. Nowadays, celebrities and famous people are more inclined to talk openly about their experience of manic depression. Public lists have been compiled naming successful artists, musicians, scientists, politicians and writers who experience manic depression. Although these lists indicate that people with manic depression can lead successful lives, they also have a tendency to romanticise the illness. These lists reinforce the view that manic depression is an illness that is experienced by people who are extraordinarily gifted.

Although there is some evidence to connect manic

depression and creativity in some people, many of us with manic depression are not gifted. Therefore, it is important that stories of ordinary people living with manic depression are also told. These stories are sometimes told to colleagues at work, or maybe to friends at the soccer club. Jan found herself talking about manic depression to strangers in the park. Through her disclosure, other hidden experiences of mental illness emerged.

> On a sunny Sunday afternoon, I was in the local park with my dog. This is a friendly park where we know all the dogs' names: Ella, Daisy, Marjong, Basil . . . Sometimes, we even know the owners' names. On this particular Sunday, I found myself walking with two older women who I had not met before. One was a retired journalist, the other a public servant.
>
> After a while, we started to talk about me. I told them that I was a lawyer who was going to take my employer to the Human Rights Commission. They were intrigued, so I explained. A few months ago, I had decided to tell the partner of my law firm that I had manic depression. This was a big mistake. For some peculiar reason, she decided to 'leak' news of my illness throughout the firm.
>
> Soon afterwards, many colleagues began to ignore me – they even stared at the carpet as they passed me in the corridor. Their nasty attitudes destroyed my self confidence and esteem. Their attitudes were far worse than the illness itself. The thing that surprised me the most about my workplace was that the people I worked with were supposedly intelligent people. It was ironic that I was rejected and marginalised by

people who were familiar with the Disability Discrimination Act.

When manic depression was mentioned, one of the women seemed quite shocked (a bit like my boss). I saw it in her facial expression, though she quickly recovered. I had seen this reaction many times before. To some, manic depression was an illness that you did not talk about – especially not in the park on a sunny Sunday afternoon to strangers!

A few days later, I bumped into this woman when we were in the park walking our dogs. She looked very earnest when she told me that she was glad to see me again. We began to walk around the park together. Suddenly, she stopped walking and began to speak to me. It was awkward; she didn't know where to start. I waited.

She wanted me to know that she has suffered from depression for thirty years. She told me about her six hospitalisations and her ECT. She was now on prozac and some other antidepressants. She told me that none of her friends knew. She had chosen to keep her illness a secret.

'Hearing you talk about your illness like it was diabetes or something, made me want to tell you about mine', she said. 'In fact, I've decided to tell some of my friends. Why should I be ashamed?'

Walking home, I reflected on the nature of social change. Would it come from a public hearing using the Disability Discrimination Act? Or was it more likely to come from encounters in the park, in the office and at the pub. I suspect both are required.

I was once told that manic depression is a bit like cancer – people don't talk about it or get too close just in case they may catch it. Once you get close to manic depression, you understand it. With every day, you fear it less.

In recent years, there has been an increase in community education about mental illness. There are public activities such as 'stop the stigma' campaigns and Mental Health Weeks. Equally important, but less noticeable, are grass-root activities in which individuals talk with each other.

Despite public education campaigns and grass-root activities, most people remain frightened and misinformed about manic depression. When people in the community realise that people with manic depression can not only get well, but also stay well, attitudes towards manic depression may improve.

Negative attitudes are also surprisingly common within the medical profession.[10] To change these attitudes, it is important that health care professionals realise that 'their patients' can get well, especially when diagnosed early and treated appropriately. This realisation may help health care professionals to improve the quality of care within the mental health system. Rather than focus only on crisis management, the focus may shift to helping people with manic depression to get on with their lives. This would involve treating 'patients' as 'people'.

As people begin their journey with manic depression, a positive approach from health professionals, families, friends, colleagues and the community is needed. A supportive environment will minimise the distress that so often accompanies the diagnosis of manic depression. When surrounded by kindness, people who are newly diagnosed are able to direct their energies into coming to terms with their illness.

Chapter 2

Beginning the journey

The journey with manic depression often begins in chaos and confusion. The journey is often unexpected, unplanned and unwelcome. In addition, people mostly begin the journey when they are unwell. To make matters worse, people with manic depression may spend years in a quagmire of misdiagnoses. The most common misdiagnoses are anxiety disorders, borderline personality disorder, attention deficit disorder, schizophrenia and clinical depression. Misdiagnoses have enormous implications for the quality of life of people with manic depression, their family and friends. Once diagnosed correctly, people with manic depression are often able to get on with their lives.

Getting the diagnosis right

With depression currently in the medical and media spotlight, health care professionals are often quick to diagnose depression and prescribe antidepressants. Sophie's tears were diagnosed as depression. She was prescribed antidepressant medication that subsequently induced an episode of mania.

Before my diagnosis, I was a workaholic with no enjoyment in anything, except work. Working long hours till I dropped, with what I then believed was burnout. When I got a little teary, I would take myself to the doctor and he would immediately prescribe antidepressants. This would cause me to wake next day with boundless energy, at times running round a local park feeling so great. If I chose not to see a doctor, I could spend days in bed waiting to recover. I now know these to have been bouts of moderate to serious clinical depression.

I believe that one of these bouts was caused by the ignorance of my local GP. I was obviously on a high and he just sent me home with some valium. I locked myself up in my bedroom for weeks. I hardly got out of bed. In the end, my Dad decided to take me off the valium. He just threw them away! I went absolutely mad. It was horrible.

My head would often race. I thought every one else understood when I complained that I could not keep up with my head. I would party all night and work all day with perhaps an hour of sleep. Many times I broke things as I raced against an unseen clock. I was aggressive and impatient, angry and intolerant of those who were slow. To be more precise, I was impatient of those who pretended they were clever. I was extremely understanding and patient with those who were intellectually disadvantaged or who had a mental illness. I have to wonder if my subconscious knew I had a disorder.

Since being diagnosed, acceptance has been one of the big things. When I feel fine, I cannot believe that anything is wrong with me. But then I hit a hump.

The humps come with stress, anxiety and overtiredness. To be honest some of the so-called 'humps' I would not have even noticed previously. But maybe I was unaware then.

I can still feel my head start to race and I start to shake. With a good night's sleep I am back to normal the next day. I can still feel depressing thoughts entering my head, and stressful situations will cause me to shed tears uncontrollably. But most of the time, I stay on top of bipolar.

To help me stay on top of bipolar, I am learning that I must say 'no' when someone wants me to do something that will cause me to rush. If I am going to face stress of any sort, I must prepare myself and tell people closest to me so as not to go at it alone. I make sure that events that may cause stress are not close together but spread out as far apart as possible. I also force myself to stick to a schedule. This includes eating, working, and bedtimes. Most importantly, I always take time out to sit and play with my dogs.

According to the professional literature, the growing awareness of the need to diagnose and treat depression contributes to the under-diagnosis of manic depression.[11] For some people, the misdiagnosis of manic depression, and the subsequent mistreatment with antidepressant medication, are life-threatening issues.

Jenny was also initially diagnosed with depression, but she was not treated with antidepressants. Whenever she felt depressed, she received professional help from a psychologist. She spent several years talking with her psychologist before switching to a psychiatrist. The psychiatrist prescribed a few different types of medications before settling on ones that gave the best results. She considers any adverse effects from her medication a small price to pay for having her life under control again. Jenny's story reinforces the importance of health care professionals looking beyond the presenting symptoms and taking a thorough history. Like many people, she only sought help when she was feeling depressed, not when she was feeling high. Her symptoms of depression caused significant distress, but feelings of euphoria were not considered a problem needing professional intervention. Feeling high was often a welcome relief from feelings of depression.

> I saw a psychologist for many years. We talked a lot about how I was feeling. But I never seemed to get any better. Finally, a friend suggested I saw a psychiatrist instead. He asked me lots of questions, not just about how I feel when I am depressed but also how I felt during other times. He asked if I had any history of manic symptoms. Feeling a bit high has always been such a relief after the relentless episodes of depression, that I never really saw these feelings as a problem. After only two sessions with the psychiatrist, I was diagnosed with bipolar disorder. He thinks I've had it for years.
>
> My psychiatrist and I tried a few different types of medications and finally settled on ones that suit me and give me results. I have some side effects from my medication (trembling and slight hair loss) but these are only a small price to pay now that I have my life back again. From being a person who would lie on a couch all day feeling no motivation and not even

bothering to shower, I gradually became 'normal' again. I have not felt symptoms of the illness for years now.

I take my medication every day as I do not want to go back 'there' again. I have a disease which requires medication for the rest of my life. Once I accepted this, I got on with living. We only have a required time here on Earth and I believe that we have an obligation to make the most of what we have. All those years of sadness and depression are lost forever, but now I have my life under control I can concentrate on the years ahead.

There are professional disagreements about the diagnosis of manic depression. While some health care professionals continue to use narrow criteria, others believe the diagnostic spectrum should be broader. Disagreements among health care professionals about the breadth of the spectrum may result in the under diagnosis of manic depression.[12]

The next two stories concern the under diagnosis of manic depression in young people. Both experienced the onset of symptoms as teenagers, but did not receive the correct diagnosis until years later. Health care professionals often find it difficult to diagnose young people with manic depression. This is sometimes due to developmental factors that may impact on the symptoms.

In the first story, health care professionals chose not to label a teenager with a psychiatric diagnosis. As a result, Lauren received no diagnosis. With her manic depression left untreated, her behaviour caused serious disruptions to herself, her fiancé and family. She was expelled from school and nearly lost her job. When she received the correct diagnosis, and recognised that her illness also affected her fiancé and family, she chose to accept treatment and avoid further disruption. Since receiving treatment, her life improved dramatically – she has been able to function efficiently at work and maintain good relationships with her family and fiancé. Lauren is now happily employed and planning her wedding.

> I am a registered nurse working with people with mental illnesses. My new workplace is very understanding about mental illness. If I need time off or need to cut back my hours they oblige. My previous employers did not know how to deal with mental illness and I was made to feel like an outcast.
>
> I have had bipolar since adolescence, but it was left untreated for a long time. Even though I had classic signs of juvenile onset bipolar disorder, the doctors did not give me a diagnosis, or any medication. Apparently, they did not want to pigeonhole my condition. So I spent my adolescence being very troublesome. I had lots of behavioural problems, mostly caused by hypomanic episodes. Not surprisingly, I was very disruptive at school. Eventually, I was expelled from school.
>
> Repeated episodes of mania and depression continued into my early twenties, but I was unable to see this at the time. My behaviour at work was deemed inappropriate and I nearly lost my job as a registered nurse. Also, my relationship with my fiancé was strained through my fluctuating behaviour.
>
> I finally found a psychiatrist who was prepared to diagnose bipolar disorder and prescribe suitable

medication for me. At first I went on and off the medication. I loved the feeling of being high and did not want to be normal. At the other end of the scale, I would get depressed and not want to live anymore. I once attempted to take my own life.

Since taking the tablets regularly, I have been able to function efficiently at work and have acceptable social skills to maintain appropriate relationships. I am now able to read my moods, as is my fiancé. I have been lucky to have a supportive fiancé and family who love me. I now realise that my behaviour affects them too.

Matthew also experienced symptoms of manic depression when he was a teenager. As a fourteen year old boy, he was misdiagnosed with schizophrenia. During the next ten years, Matthew was treated by many different psychiatrists who continued to prescribe medication for schizophrenia. As this was the wrong medication, he had several relapses. During his sixth hospital admission, the diagnosis was changed to manic depression. After enduring years of misdiagnoses and inappropriate treatments, the diagnosis of manic depression came as an enormous relief. Since commencing lithium seventeen years ago, Matthew has not experienced any episodes of illness.

My medical history in a nutshell is that from the ages of 14 to 24 I had six hospitalizations. During my first five hospitalizations, I was misdiagnosed as having schizophrenia. I had consequent relapses. On my sixth admission to hospital (17 years ago), I received the correct diagnosis. I commenced treatment with lithium and have not had an episode of illness since.

Shortly after commencing lithium, I moved out of home, and took full responsibility for my life. I started out living in a flat with a friend. Due to all my hospitalisations, many of my friends had some form of psychiatric problem. I was pondering my lot in life. I was somewhat resentful, believing that the doctors had ruined my life. They had robbed me of ten good years by misdiagnosis.

My thoughts back then were ones of litigation against medical wrongdoing. Then it dawned on me: no matter what had happened in my life, it was no skin off their nose. They were still going to drive in their flash cars, have a good life, regardless of how my life turned out. To them, I was just another patient.

I also applied similar logic to all other past relationships in my life. Even my family whom I expected more from. I began to realise that if my life was to turn around, I was the person to do something about it.

To distinguish between manic depression and schizophrenia, it is crucial for health care professionals to take a proper history, including a family history. Factors tilting the diagnosis in favor of manic depression include a family history of manic depression, an episodic course of the illness with asymptomatic phases, and periods of depression.[13]

For health care professionals to make the correct diagnosis of manic depression, they need to consider more than just the presenting symptoms. Correct diagnosis is important because people with schizophrenia, anxiety disorders and clinical depression need different treatments to people with manic depression. People also need access to different information to help them to manage these different illnesses.

Finding a suitable therapist

If misdiagnosis is suspected, it is worth seeking a second, third or even fourth opinion. It is important to get help from a competent health care professional with up-to-date training. People with manic depression choose to work with a number of different mental health professionals – psychiatrists, psychologists, general practitioners, social workers, counsellors and a range of complementary therapists. The following stories illustrate that it is sometimes necessary for people to shop around to find the right therapist. Working with the right therapist, Margaret is able to put strategies in place to help her to stay well.

> I'm 35 now. I had symptoms a fair bit when I was younger but I wasn't diagnosed until I was 28. Unfortunately, the initial diagnosis and treatment was for schizophrenia, which was a bit of a nightmare only because the medication was all wrong and the doctor was not open to changing it. I needed to change doctors to get the correct diagnosis. With the correct diagnosis and treatment, I took more control over my illness.
>
> Now that I am well, I don't underestimate how much what I think can influence what or how I feel. I need to recognise negative thought patterns, and challenge them. In particular, I need to be aware when I am vulnerable to negative thoughts. I also try to

maintain a diet with healthy foods and only moderate amounts of stimulants and alcohol. For me, alcohol is a depressant. I also do regular amounts of exercise of the enjoyable kind (not the 'should' kind like running ten miles a day). In fact, I have reduced the number of 'shoulds' in life to only the essentials. For example, I should go to work is essential, but I should cook a four-course meal for friends is not.

I have learnt my own triggers. For me, conflict is a huge problem. Others include weight/appearance, perfectionism. I am also careful to avoid getting overloaded. I make sure there is enough quiet time and that I am getting enough sleep, rest and relaxation. I am careful not to have too much stimulus. But I must also ensure that I have enough stimuli. I've found that without any stimulus, depression can quickly and easily set in.

Finally, I take medication. Taking medication for bipolar disorder is no different to taking insulin for diabetes. Medication can often help get you to a place where you can see old issues with a new perspective. In addition to getting your medications right, you should make sure you are happy with your doctor and that there is an interactive therapeutic process. I think it is very important. Also, don't be afraid to get help early if you're worried about relapse. Just make sure you get help from the right people.

Lucy was also dissatisfied with her psychiatrist. So she shopped around for a new one. It was worth it. She found a psychiatrist with whom she has good rapport and mutual respect. Together, they have built a genuine partnership. As a result of this partnership, Lucy has learnt how to manage her symptoms of manic depression more independently.

Changing psychiatrists was one of the best decisions I have ever made. My first psychiatrist was old school, I guess. In his mind, the only way to treat manic depression was to use drugs. He assumed that all his patients with manic depression were noncompliant with medication. So each time I saw him he would lecture me about taking my medication. He would just sit there and tell me what to do. There was no real communication. He just talked at me. I tried to ask him questions, but he was not terribly interested. I used to leave his office fuming. He was a risk to my mental health!

It took some time to find another psychiatrist. I did not even know how to go about looking for one. It was not something I could just look up in the Yellow Pages. Fortunately my mum had a friend who had a daughter who had a boyfriend – some weird six degrees of separation thing. Anyway, I now have a much younger woman psychiatrist whom I trust. We relate well to each other because we are at similar intellectual levels. She talks with me (not at me) and answers my questions thoughtfully. I feel like we are working as a team to learn more about my illness and how to avoid relapses. If I am worried about myself, I feel comfortable to phone and make an appointment. She has even given me her mobile number. I've never needed to use it – but it is reassuring to know that I could. I have had no sign of illness since I began working with her seven years ago. As the partnership

> grows, I have become more confident in my abilities to manage this illness.

There is a move towards genuine partnerships and mutual trust between people with manic depression and therapists. These partnerships are playing a positive role in helping people with manic depression to stay well. Within these partnerships, traditional divisions between 'us' (patients) and 'them' (professionals) are becoming increasingly blurred.

Refuting the diagnosis

Some professionals refute psychiatric labels. They do not believe that the symptoms of manic depression can be reduced to a chemical imbalance in the brain. Although there is strong evidence to indicate that manic depression is an illness that responds well to medication, some professionals prefer to treat symptoms of manic depression without drugs. When Sally was experiencing symptoms of mania, a naturopath recommended changing her diet.

> I was diagnosed with manic depression when I was 17, and was prescribed lithium. Given my strong family history, I never questioned the diagnosis. When I was in my mid-30s, my husband and I decided we wanted to have a baby. I was concerned about the effect of lithium on a baby, so I sought advice from my psychiatrist. He recommended that I stop taking lithium. Unfortunately, he did not suggest regular appointments so that he could monitor my moods.

I am not sure how long it took for my behaviour to change, but I know that my relationship with my husband did not last long enough to make a baby. He left me, and I remained off lithium.

The separation – including selling our house – was very stressful. I was quite proud of myself for staying well with so much stress in my life. I convinced myself that I must be cured. I remained off lithium.

Then, seemingly out of the blue, I became unduly obsessed about a work problem. I began having terrible dreams, waking up terrified in the middle of the night. Even though it had been eighteen years since I had experienced an episode of manic depression, I heard the mania warning bells and I sought advice. Rather than see my old psychiatrist, I chose to go to a psychologist and a naturopath for help.

The psychologist did not believe in labels such as manic depression. She convinced me that all mental illnesses are social constructions, not aberrations in brain chemistry. She recommended I took a holiday away from work. I took her advice and went down to Lorne. I spent nearly my entire life savings in less than a week. Clearly, I was still feeling manic. So I went to see a naturopath. She recommended celery juice and sardines. I now realise that I really needed lithium and sleep.

A reluctance to accept the diagnosis of manic depression is often due to a disrespect of scientific medicine and medical labels. It may also be due to lack of a definitive test, inadequate information, lack of insight or negative community attitudes. Most people who reject the diagnosis also reject treatment.

The next story is unusual because Arnold accepts treatment for manic depression, though he rejects the diagnosis.

I am a retired mayor. I was given the diagnosis of manic depression about thirty years ago, but I never accepted it.

My older brother was diagnosed with manic depression when he was a teenager. He had a psychotic episode and was locked in a psychiatric hospital for months. I've never had anything like that. I've always been very stable and successful with my work. Manic depression damaged my brother's career. Although he never talked about his illness at work, his colleagues knew. They used to gossip about it behind his back. I am quite sure he was overlooked for promotion because of his illness. Around the age of fifty, he was made redundant and has not worked since.

Looking back, I've had a few episodes of mild depression. I also had a bit of a drinking problem, and was sometimes accused of being inappropriate with women. Most of the time, I was just the life of the party. Then in 1974, I became very depressed. It came from out of the blue. I could not sleep because my thoughts were constantly racing. I was prescribed antidepressants and large doses of benzodiazepines for my insomnia. Soon after that I had an accident with the quantity of tablets I consumed. I was in intensive care for a week.

It was a terrible time for everyone. Because of my job, no-one referred to it as a suicide attempt. It was always described as 'an accident'. I even started to believe it myself.

After I recovered from my injuries, I remained on antidepressants for several weeks. Since then, I have had no symptoms of depression and have been able to enjoy a perfectly normal life. It is nearly thirty years since I have even seen a psychiatrist. My local GP has told me that I should continue taking lithium each day as a precaution. Other than that, I have not sought nor, in my opinion needed, any medical treatment for any psychological condition.

I have always queried the diagnosis of manic depression because there was only one incident that could be described as being high. I did not have highs and lows. Be that as it may, the fact remains that I resumed work in my capacity as the local mayor five months after my accident. I thereafter continued working without any difficulties, and I certainly have had no difficulty in enjoying my retirement. Needless to say, I have been able to get on with my life without having to make any changes.

It is common for people to spend some time resisting the diagnosis of manic depression. Although some people resist the diagnosis for years, angry at their psychiatrist and refusing to accept treatment, most people resist diagnosis and treatment for only a short time.[14] For many, the first crucial step to wellness is to accept the illness.

Acceptance

Rosemary believes that the sooner people accept their illness, and learn about it, the better chance they will have of managing it. Both she and her son, Jack, have manic depression. Together, they have acquired a wealth of knowledge about manic depression. Rosemary taught her son to accept the diagnosis. Jack taught his mother to feel less ashamed.

I have learnt through my own experience and through observing several other people with this illness, that the first crucial step to wellness is acceptance of the disorder. As devastating as it is to receive the diagnosis, particularly as it is almost always when you are unwell, acceptance will lead you on the road to recovery. I believe the sooner you accept your illness, and learn about it, the better chance you have of managing it. The road is long with many dangerous bends and obstacles to navigate, but with determination that road leads to a place well worth visiting.

I lead a very successful life. I have two children and work five days a week. Many people would be very surprised to know I am a sufferer of this devastating illness. I have travelled the world alone and developed a great deal of confidence since being diagnosed and medicated correctly. My trigger factors include sleep deprivation, jet-lag, hormonal fluctuations and change of seasons (spring).

My 18 year old son, Jack, also has this illness. He too is leading a very full and positive life. He graduated from high school last year and is presently studying Fine Art. He has been brought up to accept his illness and feel comfortable with having it, which has certainly helped him to cope. He is never afraid to ask for help as he feels none of the shame many sufferers feel. Although both my son and I have endured unbelievable suffering because of bipolar disorder, we both try to use this as a positive experience and truly appreciate the joy of being well. My son expresses a lot of his experiences through art.

Each day I wake up I am so very grateful for modern medication and the fact I do not have to endure the symptoms of this illness any longer. As the sufferer, you must recognise that bipolar disorder is a very dangerous illness that kills. I know because it nearly killed me. You will never be cured, but you can still lead a very fruitful satisfying life. Upon reflection it nearly destroyed me when I did not take all of this on board and I was not quite as vigilant in recognising the warning signs as I am now.

I have been diagnosed with Bipolar 2 and have experienced all three of the states that this illness can cause. By far the worst was a mixed state. Major warning signs for me that an episode is looming are an interruption of my sleep pattern. I may find it difficult to go to sleep or I may wake up in the middle of the night and have difficulty or no success in falling asleep again. Obsessive thoughts may flow and I worry about things that don't normally worry me.

An odd feeling of being cut off from myself, although only fleeting, causes concern. Before diagnosis this feeling was a prevalent sensation that continually scared me beyond belief. I was sure a descent into madness was inevitable.

I used to always put myself last and had a great deal of difficulty saying no to others' demands, which sometimes meant pushing myself too hard. This is no longer the case. When you have suffered from bipolar disorder for many years untreated, it leads to a reduction in both self esteem and self confidence, leaving you feeling you have no right to say 'no'. As a result, I used to give in to everything.

I have found it helpful to surround myself with people who know about, and are accepting, of my illness. I am quite open about it and have lots of wonderful friends, acquaintances and work colleagues who accept me in spite of it. I suppose this illness is a part of me and has made me who I am. It has taught me about compassion, about suffering, about the will to live and the desire to die. It has provided me with intoxicating highs and plummeted me into devastating lows where hope is beyond my comprehension. However it has offered me a perspective on life that most people will never have.

I treasure so much normality and the life I live today. This appreciation in turn encourages me to be vigilant about taking my medication, which is another major factor in staying well. Having a good psychiatrist, who is experienced both in treating the disorder and the pharmacology of the illness, along with regular consultations is also important. I continue with 4–6 weekly appointments even through periods of wellness. This promotes and maintains a good doctor patient relationship. Mood changes are far easier to monitor from the doctor's point of view as well as my own.

Kay Redfield Jamison's book an 'Unquiet Mind' has also been extremely helpful. Through some very difficult times I have read and reread pages from her book that have been both comforting and inspirational. Her words encouraged me when no one else could; she understood when no one else did. It is very important to know and read about others' experiences with the illness. You realise you are not the only one suffering from its cruel hand. It is so lonely when you are caught in its grip.

Only recently, I stopped sleeping, a restless unpleasant energy surfaced, and fear entered my life. I went to work because I had to. I battled through the days. I went through the motions of life, suppressing tears at various points through the day. I longed for the sleeping tablets that provided some relief until the cycling stopped. One morning, I woke up and all was well again.

Sometimes I crave sympathy for my predicament. If I broke my leg, everyone would understand, but I endure a much more deadly pain. In my mind, I bear it alone. My heart goes out to all my fellow sufferers. My psychiatrist tells me 'this is not your character, this is the illness'. I know he is right and desperately want to believe, but self doubt always creeps in.

Although people feel compassion for sufferers of physical illnesses, there is less kindness shown towards people who experience episodes of manic depression. Yet manic depression is not a character flaw, personality trait or sign of personal weakness. It is an illness.

Scientific research indicates that the cause of the illness may be genetic. Medical researchers claim that genetic understandings of manic depression will lead to improved drug treatments and screening of at-risk individuals.[15] They also claim that genetic research will improve social attitudes towards manic depression. However, knowing what causes manic depression is not the same as knowing how to live with the symptoms of the illness. In addition, molecular understandings of manic depression will not necessarily help people to behave compassionately when their friend, neighbour or relative experiences symptoms of manic depression.

Finding reliable information

People with manic depression require access to information about the illness. By learning about manic depression, people are able to take control of their lives and stay well. The next story describes a librarian with manic depression. Once correctly diagnosed, Alan searched university databases for reliable information about manic depression. Continuing to educate himself about manic depression helps him to stay in control of his illness.

> I'm 52 with a wife and 2 children. I have the illness well under control now. The hardest part for me was getting the correct diagnosis. For the first ten years, I was diagnosed with schizophrenia. As you can imagine, the medications were all wrong. I needed mood-leveller medications, not antipsychotic medication. The medication I was prescribed made my illness worse. Rather than change the diagnosis, my psychiatrist kept changing my medications and dosages. I experienced involuntary movements as an effect of all the different antipsychotic medication that he was pumping into me. I felt like his guinea pig. I endured this for over ten years. As a result, I spent my entire 20s and some of my 30s in a zombie-like-state.
>
> In my early 30s, I was admitted to hospital for the first time. It was a dreadfully traumatic experience (but

that is another story). During my admission to hospital, I was treated by a different psychiatrist. He talked with me, my close friends and family. I recall having several family meetings. He changed the diagnosis to bipolar disorder. The diagnosis actually made sense to me. It was a turning point in my life.

In hospital, I drove the nursing staff crazy with my questions about this 'new diagnosis'. It was like a new toy! The nurses did not give me much information. They just kept pushing the medical line – 'take your tablets and you will be fine'. They seemed to think the only treatment for manic depression was medication. If only it was that easy!

After my discharge from hospital-hell, I was determined to learn all I could about manic depression. I read anything I could get my hands on. In those days, there was not much information around except a few black and white pamphlets. Nowadays nearly every mental health organisation produces a glossy brochure, all with a different logo. They seem to have corporatised manic depression, but that too is another story.

Manic depression brochures and fact sheets may all look different, but the content is pretty much all the same. These brochures simply translate medical information into easy-to-read feel-good language. They are designed to help people understand the illness better. I am sure this is helpful for some people, but not me. These colourful brochures present the information as if it is black and white. They can be very patronising and prescriptive.

I now try to keep up to date by reading medical journals. I work in a library, so I have no trouble accessing these journals. The research in many psychiatric journals is a bit sloppy so I only read the articles in the well-regarded medical journals. The British Medical Journal is my favourite. These articles are much more accessible than you may think, even without specialist knowledge. For me, gaining knowledge about the illness has helped me to keep it under control. It has also made me less angry about all those years of misdiagnosis.

A few years ago, I read about an American study in which the National Depressive and Manic-Depressive Association surveyed thousands of people with manic depression. Over one third of respondents sought professional help within a year of the onset of symptoms. However, 69% were initially misdiagnosed – it is nice to know that I am not the only one! The most frequent misdiagnosis was clinical depression. Those who were misdiagnosed consulted an average of four physicians prior to receiving the correct diagnosis. Over one-third waited ten years or more before receiving an accurate diagnosis. What is so interesting about these findings is the number of people who blame their therapists. More than half believe their therapists' lack of understanding of manic depression prevented a correct diagnosis from being made earlier.

There is some fascinating literature, but you need to read it critically. Some of the research methods are questionable. A few years ago, there was a research study providing evidence that smoking marijuana helped some people to manage psychotic illnesses. This is the complete opposite to conventional wisdom about marijuana. The research was reported uncritically in the newspaper. I remember being amused when a psychiatrist wrote a letter to the paper. He was in a fury because the newspaper had published information about this controversial study. He was clearly not in favour of people making up their own minds about smoking marijuana. More alarmingly, he believed 'his patients' should only receive information about their illness from him. If 'my psychiatrist' was my only source of information about manic depression, I would not know very much at all!

My psychiatrist tells me I am better informed than him about the current medical literature on manic depression. I have also read many of the self help books on library shelves. These books give professional advice about manic depression. These self help books are usually written by mental health professionals who have deluded themselves into thinking they have all the answers.

About ten years ago, a friend gave me a book about an American professor of psychiatry, Kay Jamison, who has manic depression. Her story was different. It was genuine. She described the complexities, uncertainties and ambiguities that are so often a part of living with manic depression. At last, someone had the courage to tell the truth.

Kay's academic training gave her extraordinary insight into her own experience of illness. But it also provided a one-eyed medical view. For example, Kay believes that the major clinical problem in treating manic depressive illness is that people refuse to take medication. This is certainly not true in my case. I take the medication every day. My major problem was finding a competent clinician with the skills to diagnose my illness correctly. Once I knew what was wrong with me, I could deal with it. I have not looked back since.

People with manic depression, families and friends have a range of needs when it comes to information about manic depression. Being a librarian provided Alan with easy access to books and academic literature. Many others with manic depression do not have access, nor interest, in academic literature. Instead they rely on their psychiatrist to provide relevant information. Some may also attend formal educational sessions – health care professionals refer to these sessions as 'psychoeducation'.

Educational sessions may also be useful to family members and close friends. According to the literature, education about the illness can 'underscore the family's role in encouraging the patient to take prescribed medication and live sensibly'.[16] Unfortunately, 'psychoeducation' is predominantly seen by health care professionals as an intervention to improve patients' compliance with medication.[17] Yet education about manic depression has the potential to achieve so much more. Education about manic depression can help people to manage their illness and stay well.

Although education about manic depression provides useful information, it can be difficult to translate this information into practice. Debra is well educated about manic depression – she knows she should eat a healthy diet, drink less alcohol, avoid caffeine, exercise daily, sleep well, stay calm, and avoid conflict. However, she finds it difficult to do all these things on a daily basis. There are times when she binges on junk food and forgets to exercise. However, Debra always takes her medication.

I have tried to make my sleeping times as regular as possible. But, with my work, this is not always possible. I notice that tiredness contributes enormously to my anxiety levels and to how well I cope with other stressors.

They tell me to watch my diet. Binging on sweet and caffeinated foods is something I tend to do regularly, but I try to notice when I am struggling with things that aren't worth the trouble and cut down on those foods.

I still haven't managed to keep to a regular exercise program, but again, when I notice that things are getting to me more than they should or that I'm having trouble sleeping, I know that a half-hour walk helps to stabilise things. I have found that exercise improves so many things, so it's really only my own laziness that stops me from going for a walk every day. I have a range of excuses – it is too cold/dark in the morning, too hot to do anything, and I am far too busy.

Sometimes things in my life get a little out of control. My house is filthy, the washing builds up and I neglect bills. Alternatively, I experience extreme restlessness and recklessness with money. I have to admit that there is a very fine line between what I consider to be normal for me and a warning sign. It seems to be more about my state of mind related to the behaviours.

My way of dealing with these warning signs is to stop and look at what's going on in my life and how I'm reacting to things. I try to detach my emotions from events and situations so that I can see if my behaviour's appropriate. I try to reinforce the good behaviours that I know have a good influence on my health.

I discuss situations and my reaction to them with a trusted friend, family member or my psychiatrist. Also I've been very fortunate to find that lithium works well for me with minimal adverse effects. I may not exercise every day, or eat a balanced diet, but I always remember to take my lithium at night. It has become part of my daily routine.

There are more than 10,000 medical articles written about lithium, the medication that is commonly prescribed to treat manic depression. Many of these articles discuss patients' refusal to take lithium. Apparently, for every patient who follows the treatment course, there is at least one who does not – one who resists, protests, objects, takes too little, takes too much, or takes none at all.[18] Despite these professional problems, there is little information in the literature about why some people choose to regularly take lithium while others stop taking it.

Professionals often describe lithium noncompliance as a 'frustrating, common, and perplexing clinical problem'.[19] Yet compliance to medication is not the only 'frustrating, common, and perplexing clinical problem'. In this chapter, misdiagnosis, finding a suitable therapist and access to reliable information have been mentioned as common problems for people with manic depression. It is unclear why some health care professionals diagnose manic depression without difficulty, while others do not. However, it is clear that treatments for manic depression have the best chance of working if delivered by skilled health care professionals who are aware of current research literature and have up-to-date training.

Once correctly diagnosed, most people with manic

depression are prescribed mood stabilising medication. The next chapter will shed some light on lithium and other medications used to treat manic depression. People will discuss their reasons for taking, and not taking, mood stabilising medication. They will also discuss other treatments that people use to manage their daily lives.

Chapter 3

Choosing medication and other treatments

In September 1949, the Medical Journal of Australia published a paper by a Melbourne psychiatrist Dr John Cade. It reported the benefits of a simple salt, similar to common cooking salt, in which the metallic part is lithium rather than sodium. Since its introduction into psychiatry, lithium has gained worldwide acceptance in the treatment of manic depression. Lithium continues to be recommended as the first choice in the treatment of manic depression. The most commonly used alternatives to lithium are anticonvulsants such as sodium valproate (epilim) and carbamazepine (tegretol). Preliminary studies show that valproate and carbamazepine are of similar value to lithium. For some people, valproate and carbamazepine work better with fewer adverse effects.

The wonder drug?

For some, lithium is a wonder-drug. For some health care professionals, however, it rings alarm bells. The following story describes health care professionals who were misinformed about lithium. Their anxiety made them reluctant to prescribe lithium. In order to get prescriptions for lithium, John was forced to change doctors.

My problem is not lithium. It is other people's attitudes to lithium, especially other health care professionals. Over the years, several GPs and psychologists have been strongly opposed to me continuing to take lithium. They have told me that it is 'toxic'.

I have taken lithium since I was first diagnosed in 1972. With my strong family history, I never questioned the diagnosis. I have yearly blood tests. My level has been consistently 0.08 for as long as I can remember. My renal and thyroid function remain normal. So, personally, I do not see what all the fuss is about. I have an illness, I take a salt tablet and I get on with my life. I'm a bit overweight, but this is due to lifestyle factors, not lithium. I like beer and chips too much!

Years ago, I went to work in Cairns. The increased humidity meant I had to be careful about my lithium levels. So, upon arrival, I went to a GP. She was horrified that I had taken lithium for fifteen years. She was convinced that I must have ruined my kidneys by now. She wanted me to cease lithium and have all sorts of renal investigations. It was easier for me to just find another GP.

Over the years, several GPs and psychologists have tried to convince me to stop taking lithium. Each time, I ask them to show me evidence that lithium has all these horrible effects. To this day, I have not seen any academic article that would convince me to stop taking lithium. Recently, my psychiatrist mailed me a copy of an article – it was a systematic review of the literature on lithium. It concluded that lithium was an efficacious maintenance treatment for bipolar disorder. It was pretty convincing.

There is strong evidence that manic depression is caused by a biochemical imbalance that requires re-balancing with medication. However, some health care professionals question the evidence. A professional's attitude towards lithium will inevitably influence the way they treat people with manic depression. Those who question the role of biological factors in the cause of manic depression are unlikely to prescribe lithium.[20]

At one time it was feared that lithium treatment might lead to a decrease in renal function. However, systematically collected data indicate that even long-term treatment does not induce renal insufficiency.[21] Robert has taken lithium every day for thirty years. His mother, on the other hand, went on-and-off lithium – she stopped taking lithium whenever she felt well.

I've taken lithium for 30 years. This keeps my manic depression under control. I also have migraines. Migraines are much harder to treat – I have had to take time off work with migraines, not manic depression.

My mother also had manic depression. She would go on and off lithium. If she felt well, she did not take it. She did not like taking tablets. She was my 'anti-mentor'. Since the moment of diagnosis, I have taken my tablets every day. Sometimes I am concerned with side-effects. Nowadays I have a dry mouth and a metallic taste. I have no direct contact with a psychiatrist – my GP writes my prescriptions and organises the necessary blood tests. There is also some concern that lithium can damage kidney function. But so far, my kidneys appear to be fine.

There is no scientific evidence that lithium, when used correctly, causes renal damage. Problems can arise, however, when blood concentrations of lithium and creatinine are not closely monitored.[22] Competent health care professionals need to ensure regular blood tests.

People who are prescribed lithium are routinely informed about its possible adverse effects – thyroid and renal effects, polyuria and tremor. However, health care professionals tend to pay less attention to the other effects of lithium that may disrupt their daily lives. These effects include weight gain, decreased energy, decreased memory and concentration, and lack of enthusiasm. Judy gained an extra 25 kg in weight. Although this has implications for her self-esteem and confidence, it does not stop her taking lithium.

> I was diagnosed with bipolar five years ago. Fortunately I am happy and healthy but it has been a long road to get to this point. I was told nothing about the illness. So, for a long time I just presumed that my life would never change. I never realised that one day it might get better. I hoped that it would, but it also had my doubts. I had no confidence and very little self-esteem.
>
> I went out and educated myself about bipolar. I felt that, if I understood the illness, I would be able to understand myself. I am working as a youth worker and studying welfare. I find that my personal experiences have given me insight that is quite rare – I have been there and come out of it.
>
> Because I have been well for so long my resilience has increased. I am usually confident that I am OK. If I started to feel weird I would start taking an antipsychotic medication to prevent it from being a

full-blown episode. I have some seroquel in the bedside cupboard, just in case. This has not occurred in the past five years, so there is no reason to expect it will happen. It is good to be prepared.

I get a bit scared when I am happy. I worry that I am starting to go manic. I also worry when I experience a sad day, even though I feel confident that nothing will happen. If I've been sleeping well, taking my lithium every day, and not going out heaps, I should be safe. The key is to not push myself consistently or else I could be in trouble. Most likely I won't get sick but I can't afford to risk it.

I found that when I was able to accept the diagnosis, it made it easier for me to move on with my life. I could definitely not have gotten through it without the support of my family and friends. In my view it is almost impossible to do it alone. To treat bipolar, I take 1000 milligrams of lithium every day. I will have to take it for the rest of my life. As a result of this medication, I put on 25 kilos. I was able to lose 10–12 kilos about a year ago, but the rest will not budge. Unfortunately this is a constant reminder of the illness. If I went off lithium, I am sure I would lose the weight. But I cannot afford to do that. I've weighed up the positive and negative effects of lithium. On balance, I've decided to continue taking lithium.

Sometimes, the adverse effects of lithium can have such significant effects on quality of life that people decide to stop taking it. The major reasons for stopping lithium are weight gain, cognitive impairment, tremor, increased thirst, and lethargy.[23] In addition, some people stop lithium because they feel less sociable, outgoing, and active while taking lithium. Rather than stop medication altogether, many people who experience adverse effects of lithium choose to switch to a more suitable mood stabilising medication.

Although lithium remains the first line treatment for manic depression, alternative medication is also effective. Some who experience serious adverse effects of lithium find that valproate is equally effective without any side effects. Others use carbamazepine with good results.

The next story illustrates what can happen when a person taking lithium is not monitored properly. It led to lithium toxicity, renal failure and a parathyroid gland tumour. Despite these serious adverse effects, Marjorie did not stop taking medication altogether. Instead, she commenced new mood stabilising medications. This medication suited her much better and gave her a new lease of life.

I'm 53. I've had this illness for over 30 years. I think my wilder days as a musician may have sparked this illness. I sang in Hair and Jesus Christ Superstar. I also used drugs (especially marijuana). We all did back then. I think smoking pot sparked my illness. I was put on lithium. I took it for 20 years. As a result I now have renal failure. I also have a parathyroid gland tumour. These are the effects of high blood concentrations of lithium.

The problem was that I was not properly monitored when I was taking lithium. My GP wrote my prescriptions but did not observe me closely. He did not monitor by blood levels. I had irregular blood tests – hardly any, in fact. I was not told the signs of lithium toxicity. So how could I have recognised myself having lithium toxicity?

I have since been told that a serious lithium overdose can be fatal. I now realise that I had nearly all the classic signs of lithium poisoning: nausea, drowsiness, dizziness, mental dullness, confusion, blurred vision and slurred speech. Thank goodness it did not give me muscle twitching or an irregular heartbeat.

I changed my doctor just in time. My new doctor saw the signs of lithium toxicity and quickly ceased lithium. He switched me to tegretol ten years ago. My life changed overnight. I felt clearer and sharper. I did not want to just sit on the couch anymore. The entire twenty years that I had been taking too much lithium, I had just sat around on a couch. I had zero energy. I literally had not socialized for twenty years – except with mum and dad.

After starting tegretol, I became more gregarious, and started to take an interest in my appearance. I am now 'up' most of the time. I moved out of mum and dad's home seven years ago and bought my own place. I have gone back to my music and am now learning to sing acapella. It's great, but I still prefer rock and roll music.

I have a close circle of friends and good family support. I spend most of my time with people who don't have mental illnesses. Years ago, I joined a support group – I found it very boring. I did not want to sit around, drink coffee and smoke with other people with a mental illness. However, I met some musicians in the support group. We formed a band and performed together for two years.

I periodically do paid work but I prefer to be on the disability pension. Paid work puts undue stress on me.

Even though I don't have a full-time job, I have lots of projects.

I am always mindful of manic depression and aware of where I am at. I do not touch marijuana. In fact, I don't take risks of any sort. We have a chemical thing happen in our brains. So you need to watch out that you don't get on the wrong tram. It is a long way back from a breakdown. A breakdown is a huge thing. So I don't fool around with my medication.

From all reports, the mental health system is much worse today than in my days at Royal Park. At least they kept me in hospital until I was well. Nowadays they kick you out after only a few days. I would hate to get sick today . . . and I am not going to be!

I get early warning signs. I call them flashes of mental illness. I think someone who is using a mobile phone is talking to me. So, if I feel a little over the edge, I take half a valium. If I am not asleep by 2 am (head buzzing with ideas, or thinking about something stressful), I take a sleeping tablet. I call these sleeping tablets my 'emergency drugs'. I take my emergency drugs about once a month.

Emergency drugs

Many people with manic depression are vigilant about sleep because sleep deprivation can trigger an episode of illness. Professionals advise patients to avoid situations likely to disrupt sleep routine.[24] However, daily disruptions in life are sometimes hard to avoid. In these 'emergency' situations, sleeping tablets may be useful.

Rather than take a regular daily dose of lithium, Virginia

is prescribed only sleeping tablets. She takes these short acting hypnotics from time-to-time, whenever she feels 'warning signals'.

I am 37. I work full-time and am also studying psychology part-time. I was diagnosed at 31, but looking back I've probably had it since I was a teenager. I need to be honest with myself about the illness. What I have is for real and I cannot make it go away. Avoidance behaviour does not work. I cannot run away from it.

I used to take lithium and then epilim, but my psychiatrist took me off them. It is better for me just to take sleeping tablets from time to time. I get my prescriptions from my local GP. To stay well, I watch my sleep patterns like a hawk. For me, sleep is the crucial ingredient in treating my illness. So, if I am not sleeping well, I take a sleeping tablet. Other things that are important are diet (I avoid too much junk food) and exercise. I avoid negativity, especially people who drain my energy. I have strong family support and my partner will tell me if he thinks I am not well. I listen to friends and partner if they say 'are you OK?' I pay attention to little things.

When I am becoming unwell, my sleeping patterns change. I have learnt to control this with a sleeping tablet. If I let it slide, I can't stop it and I become unwell. The secret for me is to not let it slide. So, to prevent an episode, I exhaust myself on my exercise bike for two hours, then sleep. If I slide further, I go and see my GP. I do not want to become sick, so I take it very seriously.

There is evidence that sleep deprivation can induce episodes of mania[25]. The underlying causes of sleep deprivation are diverse. Emotional reactions such as anger, infatuation, grief, and fear can cause insomnia. Sleep reduction also occurs with shift work, social events, jet lag and excess caffeine. Although it is not always possible to avoid the triggers of sleep deprivation, it is possible to monitor sleeping habits and intervene with a sleeping tablet when necessary. Sometimes, however, a sleeping tablet is not enough. It may be necessary to also take a low dose of antipsychotic medication.

Finding suitable treatments

It was difficult for George to find suitable treatment. After being prescribed many different combinations of medications, with many unpleasant effects, he eventually sought another medical opinion. His new psychiatrist prescribed more suitable medication. George also discovered a range of other therapies that help him to stay well.

> I was diagnosed with bipolar about six years ago. Medication is the most important ingredient for me to stay well. To be more precise, the right medication at the right dose. The initial two years of trial and error with many different combinations of medication were horrific. Not only was I coming to grips with the trauma of being diagnosed with a mental illness, my first psychiatrist put me on a concoction that was far from suitable. From there, it was a further year or two and several further experiments with other drugs until

we settled upon epilim and cipramil which still left me with a few major adverse effects. I do not understand why health professionals refer to these effects as 'side-effects'. The unpleasant effects are directly related to taking the drug. Naturally, people who experience unpleasant effects from medication are more likely to want to cease the medication. If you stop taking the drug, the effects (both wanted and unpleasant) will stop.

It wasn't until I changed doctors that we hit upon a medication, avanza, which had been developed several years ago. It has been fantastic. Apart from a dry mouth, there were virtually no other adverse effects. It has kept my mood relatively elevated and regulated my sleep.

Another key factor has been the reduction of alcohol. I had adopted a pattern of binge drinking from the age of sixteen which involved going out on most weekends with mates and partying. I had no idea that this constituted binge drinking. However I would more often than not end up quite drunk which in my situation could be quite detrimental. The challenge of reducing my alcohol consumption, and socialising without alcohol, was truly great. However, I firmly believe now that this has helped me become stable and, more importantly, stay stable.

The idea of taking up yoga came from an article I read in a magazine. Ironically, I was waiting to see my Psychiatrist! I hadn't been doing much exercise apart from a game of golf on the weekend and the article triggered some interest. Well it wasn't long before I found a book for beginners in Hatha Style yoga and started to practise a little each week. From there

I have joined a class and taken up meditation which became a natural progression and haven't really looked back.

The benefits of yoga have been terrific. It brought about a feeling from within me that wanted to take better care of myself with more exercise, better diet and grooming. It sort of helped get in touch with the inner me. The other obvious benefits were a more flexible and supple body and in turn a better mood.

The meditation has also brought about changes that have been surprisingly beneficial. Regular practise has been critical in developing my thought patterns. In some way, I have been able to readily block any thoughts that I recognise to be somewhat negative and/or irrational. The other benefits have been my mood is generally better the next day. I am able to think more clearly and I find myself more relaxed and less anxious.

About a year ago, my GP suggested that I went and saw yet another psychologist that specialised in anxiety and depression. He recognised that my anxiety levels had been quite high for many years, partly due to the uncertainty of having a mental illness. Through cognitive behavioural therapy, we were able to modify my thought patterns that were detrimental and identified and worked through other issues of concern.

It would have been incredibly helpful if I had seen this person soon after I was diagnosed. We identified that the stigma of bipolar had an incredibly deep adverse effect on my self confidence, self image and my major fear and uncertainty of what my life was going to be like.

The last couple of years have seen me complete my

studies and I have been lucky enough to find some regular casual work as a courier driver and labourer. Looking back, the fact that I have had some form of work that has kept me busy as well as the goal of completing my studies was crucial in keeping me stable.

Although medication is often an important component of treatment, there are many other therapies that also contribute to people with manic depression staying well. These other complementary therapies include diet, exercise, yoga, meditation, dog walking and cognitive-behavioral therapy. It is often a matter of finding what works best for each individual person.

Complementary treatments

People with manic depression use a range of complementary therapies, often in conjunction with prescribed medication. The next story describes Julie working cooperatively with a psychiatrist and naturopath.

I am a 26 year old woman. I have a full-time job as a physiotherapist and was married last year. I started taking lithium when I was sixteen. I have always complied with my psychiatric medication, even though I am aware that I have choices. My 78 year old great aunt who also has manic depression has stayed well for over thirty years by using brewers yeast. She believes that one teaspoon per day of brewers yeast has the same effect on her as lithium.

Taking medication is only a small part of what I need to do to stay well. My wellbeing also depends on a range of social activities. I get a lot of pleasure from my friends. For the past five years, a group of university friends and I have subscribed to the Melbourne Theatre Company. I am also a member of a monthly book club. I work in a large public hospital where the hospital managers often drive me completely crazy. So I treat myself to a weekly shiatsu massage.

I've always believed that exercise is fundamental to my health. I still play competition tennis – I started playing competition when I was twelve. My main form of transport is a bicycle – I cycle to work every day. I also take my golden retriever for long walks along the Yarra in the morning, and a quick walk at night. My neighbour and I have recently started Tai Chi lessons. We are hopeless, but it is fun.

I also believe that my diet affects my moods. When I am lacking nutrients, I feel more moody. A naturopath helped me with my diet – he recommended that I ate mainly organic food, which I do. He also recommended that I take Vitamin B and Omega-3. He sometimes administers naturopathic detoxification strategies to reduce my level of toxins (e.g. heavy metals and chemical residues). If I am a bit run down, he also administers a homeopathic constitutional and stress reduction formulae to reduce the biological impact of my internal stressors. I recently had my hair analysed for trace elements.

I have developed a lifestyle that suits me and keeps me well. A friend who lives in Byron Bay treats his manic depression quite differently. He chooses not to take medication. Instead, he uses Traditional Chinese Medicine, herbs, aromatherapy and reiki. It works for him. Like me, he has not had a relapse for over ten years. I think the secret is to find what works for you, and stick to it.

My husband and I are planning to start a family next year. My psychiatrist and naturopath have agreed to work together to help me to stay well.

For health care professionals to recommend complementary therapies, they require scientific evidence to determine their usefulness. Most complementary therapies have not been scientifically studied and their effects on manic depression are not fully understood. Omega-3 fatty acids (found in fish oils) are currently being studied to determine their usefulness for long-term treatment of manic depression. St John's Wort is also being studied in regard to depression. There is some evidence that it may reduce the effectiveness of some medications. It may also react with some prescribed antidepressants or cause a switch to mania.[26]

The lack of scientific evidence does not necessarily discourage people with manic depression from trying these therapies. People with manic depression often stick with what works for them, with or without scientific evidence.

Miraculous cure

When people with manic depression feel well, it is easy to mistakenly believe in misdiagnosis, or miraculous cure. Michelle learnt to take medication, even when she thinks she no longer needs it.

In the past, when I felt well, I used to believe that I was cured, or that there was never really anything wrong with me in the first place. I would stop taking my medication. I now realise that I need to take my medication, no matter how much I sometimes believe I no longer need it.

I have been well for the past three years, and have an amazing life as the mother of two children and also working as a musician and music teacher, whilst studying full time. For me, staying well depends on a number of things that are in my control. First, I now take the medication, even when I feel well. I also need to exercise on an almost daily basis. I avoid drinking alcohol, as this always seems to affect the balance I seem to be able to achieve without it. I sometimes have to acknowledge that I am not getting enough sleep. I convince myself that whatever I feel I have to do can really wait another day. Sleep at that particular time is more important.

The early signs that things are going wrong are when I begin to stay up later and later, completing projects that I feel have to be finished immediately. I start saying 'yes' to things that I don't really want to be involved in. I volunteer myself for many committees and charity groups – I over commit myself. I begin to feel panicky. My mind starts to race. I begin to look for/think of ways of escaping.

To prevent an episode of illness, I need to recognise the early signs (which these days I mostly do) and then I remind myself of where I have been, and where I could be heading again if I don't start looking after myself and my needs. It also helps that my husband, after a number of years of bad experiences, is able to recognise the most subtle of signs and has learnt how to gently remind me of what these signs could mean.

There is now substantial clinical evidence which supports continuing to take lithium, even when feeling well. However, it has taken many years of research to convince health care professionals that maintenance lithium can lessen the frequency and severity of episodes of illness.[27]

Peter chooses to take a low dose of lithium. He only increases the dose when he feels 'warning signals'. These warning signals are mild symptoms that may indicate an impending episode of mania or depression.

I used to work as a political advisor. I got out due to the stress. The important thing for me is to be 'aware' of my mood states. If I am 'aware' then it is relatively easy to stay in control of the situation before it gets out of hand. I try to live within normal bounds. Instead of flying off like Icarus into the sky, I prefer to stay down on the earth.

Normally, I maintain regular bed times. It is important for me to get up at the same time each morning. When I am high, my regular bedtime is broken and all-nighters become the norm. During these periods, I will often start writing a brand new story, one of ambitious scope, which never seems to get finished. I am passionate about writing. I think my writing helps me to stay grounded and explore many of the issues that I have in my life through the narrative process. It also helps me when I am experiencing turbulent emotions to read books about people with bipolar (most notably Kay Redfield Jamison's 'Touched With Fire'). Reading these books seems to put me in touch with the reality of the illness and to not try and romanticise or forget how serious it really is.

When things are starting to go wrong, I can't stop speaking and ideas are rapidly flowing into my mind. I say and do things, which are humorous to me, but hurtful to other people. I have so much energy. If work is the problem, I try to avoid stress and put myself into a calmer environment. I also make sure I get plenty of exercise (walking) to help burn off all my excess energy.

If I feel myself getting too energetic or flighty, I will dose up on lithium. Instead of taking three tablets I will up the dose to four. Just until I feel myself righted, and in balance again. I also talk to my psychiatrist. It is important to discuss any measures I intend to take with a competent physician.

People with manic depression often take control of their medication, particularly when they feel slightly off balance. However, little is known about whether age and sex factors are involved in people's decisions to alter their medication. For example, do young men adjust their lithium dose more than older women?

Health care professionals describe people who stop taking medication as 'non-compliers'. They believe that non-compliance with medication is 'notoriously common' among people with manic depression.[28] However, there is little information in the literature about how many people with manic depression stop taking medication, for what reasons they stop, for how long, and at what point in their journey.[29]

Most people who contributed stories to this book take medication – some describe taking it 'religiously'. Medication is an important part of their stay well strategy. Some health care professionals recommend 'lithium holidays'. Lithium holidays are intended to reduce the long-term side effects of lithium by giving the body's systems an opportunity to recover from sustained exposure to the drug. Mixed results have been reported – some people are able to sustain longer holidays without relapse; others relapse quickly.[30] Susan describes an extended lithium holiday.

> I took lithium for over twenty years. During this period, I finished my medical degree and specialised as a surgeon. My family are very proud – there are not many female surgeons in our health care system. In the past five years, I have settled into a long-term relationship with my partner, bought a house together and started to nest.
>
> About four years ago, my psychiatrist and I decided to cease my medication. I am much more settled in my work, social and private life. This decision appears to have worked well. I have been on a 'lithium holiday' for four years. It seems I am one of the lucky ones. I did not experience a rapid relapse after lithium withdrawal.
>
> On occasions, when my mood appears to be unsettled, my girlfriend suggests I make an appointment to see my psychiatrist. I trust her judgment. Normally, we just go away for a few days – getting away from the pressures of work usually does the trick. If I am agitated about work, my psychiatrist recommends I take sleeping tablets and an anti-psychotic for a few

days. I recently asked about going back on lithium, but he is happy that I am doing OK. I trust his judgment. Plus I have great support at home.

During her lithium holiday, Susan continued to see her psychiatrist. However, some people choose to take permanent lithium holidays against medical advice. Rather than take prescribed medication, Luke manages his illness with 'brain food', self discipline, and marijuana. With his treatment regime, he has not had an episode of illness for seven years.

I am married with two kids. I work as a finance broker. I was diagnosed in 1997 after being caught by the police jogging at 3am. It would not have been worth mentioning except that I was completely naked. At the time, I thought I was someone important, God or something. They immediately put me on lithium. At first lithium was OK. I no longer wanted to take off naked down the main street – this was a good thing. But after a few months, my brain felt dulled, and I lost all my creativity. I felt it was killing me. I knew there were other drugs that I could try, but I decided to try to manage the illness myself.

I read about bipolar on the internet. There is an enormous amount of information on the internet – it becomes quite repetitive after a while. I surfed the internet and learnt enough to manage my symptoms and stay well. I have learnt to keep my highs under control. I choose to play in the middle. Years ago, I played footy for Carlton. I had some of the best life coaches. I learnt about nutrition, body, and self discipline. I leant to be strong in both body and mind.

I choose not to take any prescribed medication. Instead, I use brain food (omega 3, nuts and Japanese food). I also use marijuana. Pot is time out for reflection. It helps me to keep my stress under control. I know the experts say that marijuana is harmful for people with psychotic illness, but it works for me. Maybe I am the exception. Who knows?

Another thing that has helped me to manage stress is to get more organized. Rather than keep pages and pages of notes, I carry an appointment diary. This helps me not to take too much on. Also, being more disciplined with my time. I have learnt to balance work, family and self. My partner helps to keep me level. She has a mood stabilising influence on me! Sometimes she is ruthless. I no longer make decisions on my own.

All the things I have read on the internet stress the importance of sleep. For me, sleep is not hugely important. Meditation and exercise are more important. When I am feeling depressed, I walk, run, push weights, kick box, dig in the garden. I burn energy while working out how to solve whatever is bothering me. When I feel depressed about a problem, smoking pot allows me to focus my mind. When feeling high, I take time out. I meditate. I talk with my partner about how I am feeling. I do not allow myself to get really high.

Although no study has determined the incidence of manic depression in people who use marijuana, it is believed that marijuana can contribute to episodes of manic depression.[31]

In particular, there is anecdotal evidence linking marijuana and initial episodes of psychotic illnesses including manic depression. Many people with manic depression choose to stop smoking marijuana because they believe it contributes to episodes of their illness.

Chris also smoked marijuana, but only when he was a patient in hospital. Since discharge from hospital, he chooses to manage his illness without marijuana. Chris prefers non-pharmacological strategies to help him live with manic depression.

I see a psychologist every week. I'm happy to pay $70 per week for someone to listen and help me work through my problems, including my work stress. It is so much more helpful than the doctors and nurses in hospital. The only treatment I received in hospital was drugs. I was forced to take their medication. If I refused, they would inject it into me. I was also given a lot of marijuana – by the other patients, not the staff. It helped to pass the time in hospital. After my release, I made my own decisions – I have not touched marijuana or prescription medication since discharge. And I never will.

My psychologist only works with people who are not taking medication (this includes marijuana). His approach requires me to be alert and mentally engaged. He does not believe in medicating chemical imbalances in the brain. He believes in changing the behaviour that causes the chemical imbalance in the first place. He calls it cognitive behavioural therapy, but I see him more like my personal coach. He helps me to attain my personal best in all areas of my life.

My psychologist will tell me if he thinks I am losing it. He encourages my creativity. When I was in hospital, the medicos labelled my positive ideas as 'grandiose'. They put a label on everything. I had 'illusions of grandeur' and 'pressured speech'. In my mind, I had ideas and energy to burn. They chose to sedate me. My psychologist thinks I should burn my energy off. So now, if I wake up at 4am with energy, I take my cat out for a walk.'

In the treatment of manic depression, psychological therapy is recommended as an 'adjunctive' therapy, an optional extra. It has been shown that psychological therapy can have good results when used in conjunction with mood stabilising medication. In particular, cognitive behavioural therapy (CBT) has helped many people to have less frequent episodes of illness.[32]

Psychological therapy can help people with manic depression to recognise, and deal with, their early warning signs. Learning to identify early signs of illness is an important stay well strategy. People with manic depression also need to develop insight into factors that may trigger an episode of illness. Insight into triggers and warning signs are an important part of most stay well plans.

In addition to finding suitable medication and complementary therapies, people with manic depression develop many interesting and varied strategies to stay well. These strategies will be explored further in the next chapter. Although many people with manic depression hope for an instant recovery, it usually takes time, sometimes years, to develop the experience and wisdom to control the illness. It is often not as simple as medicating and moving on.

Chapter 4

Being mindful of manic depression

People with manic depression develop an awareness of factors that may trigger an episode of illness. These 'triggers' include sleep deprivation, shift work, fatigue, jet lag, hormonal fluctuations, change of seasons, stress, grief, all night partying and recreational drugs. It is possible to avoid some triggers, but not others. So it is necessary for people with manic depression to develop an awareness of individual warning signs. These are physical, mental, emotional changes that may indicate the onset of an illness. Many people with manic depression have tell-tale warning signs such as changes in sleep and mood. Others experience unique early warning signs.

Amy has both tell-tale and unique warning signs. She responds quickly to these warning signs to ensure she avoids episodes of illness. Her interventions involve sleep and long walks on the beach. Occasionally she needs to make an appointment with her psychiatrist. Although she would prefer to forget about her illness and just get on with her life, she benefits from maintaining an awareness of her illness. Mindfulness helps her to develop strategies to manage the illness and avoid relapses.

I was diagnosed with manic depression when I was 19 years old. Between the ages of 19 and 25, I was hospitalised twice with mania, and twice with catatonic psychotic depression. My ups and downs were pretty drastic. With lithium, my mood swings are now manageable. I have not had a relapse for 16 years. After my last episode, I went back and finished my Arts degree. I now work as a journalist.

My experiences within the mental health system were horrific, so I choose to look outside the mental health system for ways to stay well. I have never attended group or family therapy, nor needed psychosocial rehabilitation. I avoid support groups. Instead, I rely on a range of less institutionalised strategies to stay well. In my early 30s, I sat down with a few close friends to develop a 'crisis intervention plan'. I gave them each a copy of the document. Thankfully, I've never needed to use it.

The secret for me is to be mindful that I have an illness. As much as I'd like to forget about it, I realise that it is not going away. So I need to be aware how my mind and body are responding to things that are happening in my life. When I feel good, my illness is in the back of my mind. It does not play a large role in my life, but I am aware of its presence. When I feel a bit down or high, I become slightly more vigilant. Sometimes I need to intervene by having a few good sleeps or a walk along the beach. Every now and then, I feel concerned enough to make an appointment with my psychiatrist.

Over the years, I have found sexual attraction a major trigger. Whenever I start a new relationship, I have this amazing technicolour experience. It's a lot like being manic. I get this amazing feeling – I want to have sex all day and night. It is fun for a while, and my boyfriends seem to enjoy it. But if it goes on for too long, I must intervene. In my stay well plan, sleep is more important than sex.

I also find working for large organisations and bureaucracies a trigger. I become stressed when I have to work with people who do not share my values. Unfortunately, as a journalist, this happens quite often. When I get stressed, my mind races. I often become flushed in the face and I start to perspire heavily. When this happens, it is a sign that I need to have some quiet time. For me, quiet time means no external stimulation: no TV, radio, newspapers. Being a luddite, with no technology, helps me to find my balance. I do nothing except take long quiet walks, eat healthy foods and sleep. It normally takes a weekend to recover from a stressful event at work. I tried to get into meditation and spiritual stuff. But I was bored stiff. I also tried yoga, but my joints are too stiff. Incidentally, I also make lots of puns when I am getting high.

I must be particularly careful of stress and sleep deprivation. In some cases, stress causes disruption to my sleep because I wake up in the middle of the night thinking about some work problem. I self-medicate and go back to sleep. I used to consider needing to take a sleeping tablet as a sign of weakness. Now I see it as part of my stay well package.

Sometimes, a few late nights cause me to become overly sensitive and I over-react to work and other life stresses. At these times, I clear my social calendar for a few nights and chill out. My friends are very understanding about my need to do this occasionally.

My psychiatrist does not have a very high profile in

my stay well package. I see him once a year. I always make the appointment around my birthday, so I remember. Every year, he begins by asking me whether I am in a relationship. I may surprise him one year and say 'yes'. We chat a bit, and then he writes a prescription for lithium and arranges a blood test. These visits usually take about 15 minutes. I get most of it back on Medicare, so it really is a cheap illness for me to manage. If I need extra scripts, I organise them through the receptionist. I have developed a nice relationship with the receptionist.

My friends are more instrumental in helping me to stay well. If I am feeling a bit stressed, I contact a friend to talk things through. It never crosses my mind to talk things through with my psychiatrist. My friends know me well; my psychiatrist only knows my illness well.

Every now and then I stumble into an event that is really, really stressful. This happened last year when my German shepherd was diagnosed with bone cancer. I rang my psychiatrist's receptionist. She slipped me in between clients so that I could see him. There wasn't much to say except I was very stressed. I needed something stronger than temazepam to get me to sleep through the night. My psychiatrist suggested I take half a respiridol and two temazepams. The meeting took less than ten minutes but it helped me to get a good night's sleep. He asked me to phone in a week to let him know how I was going. I phoned the receptionist to tell her my beloved dog had been put down. I also told her that I was travelling OK. I only needed to take the sleeping medication for a few days, but it is reassuring to know it is there for another rainy day.

With warning signs, it is important to intervene quickly to avoid experiencing a relapse. Health care professionals refer to this as 'self management'. Research has shown that learning to 'self manage' manic depression is an invaluable part of stabilising the condition.[33] Teaching people to recognise early warning signs has been shown to reduce the number of relapses.

The term 'self management', however, is somewhat confusing because it gives the impression that people manage their illness alone. This is not the case. The challenge for people with manic depression is to take responsibility of their chronic illness. 'Self management' includes a willingness to access the assistance of others when required. Most importantly, self management involves an awareness of trigger factors, early warning signs, and the ability to intervene effectively to prevent an episode of illness.

Awareness

By paying attention to little things – small changes in sleep patterns, energy levels, moods, thoughts, speech, spending habits – Damien is able to nip symptoms of manic depression in the bud. Although he is mindful of warning signs, he does not obsess about them. He accepts a few bad days, knowing that they do not necessarily signal an episode of illness. However, Damien knows when it is necessary to intervene. His self management plan includes keeping antipsychotic medication (olanzapine) handy at the bedside and in his wallet. When necessary, he does not hesitate to take it.

Let me give you a few tips of how I stay well with bipolar after ten years 'in the game'. I take it seriously and not too seriously at the same time. I need to be very conscientious about my commitment to taking my medication and turning up for appointments with psychiatrists and psychotherapists. I also need to be informed on broad issues surrounding bipolar. But at some point, I must loosen the tag on my forehead that says 'bipolar' and just get on with it. Otherwise I become obsessed about my disease and then I become my disease.

It is so easy to become a disease that happens to be human, rather than a human that happens to have a disease. So its an essential Zen paradox: take it seriously and not seriously at the same time.

I think too much. A few years ago, I started meditating. Meditation is great to still my mind. Also, a regular massage reduces stress levels and keeps me centred within my body. Regular exercise is great – it gets the serotonin levels right and once again, I feel 'in my body' and the fresh air and sunlight can only do good. I also try to do at least one thing a week to have fun/make me laugh. Even went to a laughter club, which felt odd but was actually very funny!

Using a spiritual, not religious, approach, I ask myself 'what is this illness teaching me about myself?' rather than 'why have I been singled out by God to be punished like this?' In fact, my illness, through much psychotherapy, has taught me bucket loads about myself and the lenses through which I see the world. This would never have happened if I hadn't have got bipolar. It's not exactly that I would recommend having bipolar as a route to self understanding and acceptance, but, what the hell, they were the cards I was handed.

I had to make great changes between who I thought I was and who I actually was (and who I had become through the illness). This has been hard stuff. Pre-illness I was a high flying corporate lawyer. Now I am not, but I still hold on tightly at times to past illusions of great social status (or was it grandiosity?). Wellness for me comes when I can accept the bald truth of who I am – what I do for a living, where I live, how many friends I have. Sanity is about being squarely rooted in reality! Then I can breathe easily.

Staying mentally well also means looking after my other physical illnesses. It can be easy to sideline my asthma and bad back for example, because my bipolar seems the be-all-and-end-all. Yet if I don't regularly attend to the asthma and back, I can get myself in a pickle, because not only do those physical complaints flare up, they have an effect on my mood state.

I have early signs of things going wrong. These include sleeping too much, losing appetite and drooping (!) libido. On the manic side, repeatedly not sleeping well, incredible confidence with women (I'm normally pretty shy around them), lots of creative ideas that are not fully acted upon, probably acting as if I was drunk. For instance, I might lose my inhibitions and say things to people – forgetting the social niceties of what happens when you say socially 'unnice' things to people which you just think are authentic and true.

I have learnt ways to prevent episodes of illness. I always have zyprexa (antipsychotic medication) handy at my bedside or in my wallet to nip the first signs of mania in the bud. My psychiatrist is OK about me taking it when I think I need it. He trusts me to be responsible with it. I've only taken zyprexa twice in the past year. When I feel a bit high, my first line treatment is herbal tea. Mostly, herbal tea does the trick.

To stay well, I try to have a 'normal', fairly 'humdrum' simple rhythm to life. I eat/sleep/go to work at more or less the same time (opposite to wild rhythmic disturbances of bipolar). Staying well also depends on a small tight-knit group of support friends who I talk things through with when things are starting to go haywire. I also accept that there are some times when the best I can do is 'doona therapy' – batten down the hatches until the mood passes. I have a fridge magnet that says 'Next Mood Swing 6 minutes'. Unfortunately, my low moods last a bit longer than that.

In the medical literature, the 'early' symptoms of depression are listed as mood change, psychomotor change, increased anxiety, appetite change, suicidal ideation and sleep disturbance. The 'early' symptoms of mania are listed as sleep disturbance, psychotic symptoms, mood change, psychomotor change, appetite change and increased anxiety. Studies show that teaching people to recognise early symptoms of depression and mania may prompt early intervention.[34] However, the symptoms listed in the medical literature are late, not early, signs. Intervention is required long before suicidal ideation, psychotic symptoms and increased anxiety are present.

When Clara notices certain behavioural changes, she seeks help from her psychiatrist. However, she often needs to wait for an appointment. If the situation is serious enough, she contacts her GP. Clara also finds telephone counsellors helpful. As a single woman with minimal other support, phone counselling provides bridging support until her psychiatrist is available.

I've had manic depression for at least fifteen years, though I only became aware I had the condition in my twenties. I knew that something was definitely 'wrong' with me. I often experienced quite extreme mood swings, which also set off some impulsive behaviour.

Over the past few years, I've become more familiar with manic depression, and become more knowledgeable about my illness in particular. I've finally developed strategies for dealing with my problems.

I often carry a lot of tension and pent-up emotion inside. To stay well, I need to let out steam. I do this by writing a letter or journal entry, exercising regularly, getting lots of sleep and rest, allowing myself time for fun and recreation, eating properly and taking vitamin supplements.

I am now quite experienced and knowledgeable about the many facets of my illness. I've learned to recognise the many tell-tale signs of 'going off the rails'. These include increased periods of significant anxiety and depressive thinking. This type of thinking tends to form a negative, vicious cycle. It results in lowering my self-confidence and mood.

Often, triggers are external events occurring around me. Either directly or indirectly, these events upset and/or depress me. If enough of these triggers occur in a relatively short space of time – say a few weeks – then I know that I'm vulnerable to an extreme mood swing. Since taking anti-depressants and mood stabilisers, it is more likely to be depression than mania.

If I see a mood swing on the horizon, I seek help. First, I usually ring and make an appointment with my psychiatrist. However, I invariably need to wait a few weeks or so before I can see him. So, if the situation is serious enough, I'll see my GP instead. I also seek whatever support I can from the outside world. I contact friends and my sister (who is able to give me support online, despite the impersonal nature of email!) and miscellaneous other sources including university and telephone counsellors.

Unfortunately, my support sources are somewhat limited, coming from a small family with parents who are not able to be emotionally supportive. I am also single, but have a few very close friends who I can rely on most of the time to lend me a kind ear. Sometimes they aren't available, in which case I ring Lifeline, who provide an excellent telephone counselling service staffed by volunteers.

In the medical literature, it is assumed that people with manic depression will not achieve 'remission' for any significant length of time.[35] In contrast to this professional pessimism, many contributors have not experienced a relapse for over ten years, some much longer. With effective treatment, people with manic depression can achieve complete and sustained 'remission' for significant lengths of time. Martin is one such example. With his 'little therapies', he has remained well for the past fifteen years.

I was diagnosed with the disorder 25 years ago and my last relapse was 15 years ago. I think that many things may have contributed to helping me stay well such as maturity, luck, courses in yoga, meditation, relaxation, newer classes of antidepressants, working in interesting short term part-time jobs away from the corporate bull. I also have a few 'wet weather' friends who will listen and stand by me in bad times.

I have developed some personal 'little therapies' which I believe help me to manage the illness. I do all the usual stuff like regular balanced meals, minimal alcohol, and exercise. I make sure I get enough rest, including time to veg out. I take the medication without fail – no ifs, buts, even when feeling good. I vary my drugs only after review with my GP and psychiatrist. I keep scripts up-to-date. Also, I arrange suitable timing of blood tests for lithium level, thyroid and renal function and their interpretation.

I have a good relationship with both my GP and psychiatrist. If I want to try complementary therapies, I discuss it with them first. Twenty five years after diagnosis, I eventually sought opinions and treatments from other psychiatrists and sleep disorder specialists. This proved to be successful and improved things for me.

If I am feeling high or low, I distract myself by doing physical or mental work. Doing something useful, even if trivial, seems to help. I continue to try to desensitise myself from things that push my buttons. I try not to get angry, particularly at myself. It can be very difficult for me to determine if high spirits, quick wit, creation of hilarity and entertainment for friends is evidence of a bright personality or crossing the line into low level mania. If a high is suspected, I check with my wife.

If a low is developing, I take a weekend away, take prescribed sleeping medication, one or two nights consecutively. I see my GP or psychiatrist if the episode does not improve. If I feel that an episode of illness is looming, I try to postpone as many decisions as I can. I make sure I do not sell my house or car or buy another house or car. I do not leave my job or suddenly start a new one. I do not travel overseas.

Life changes

To stay well, most people with manic depression make some lifestyle changes. These may be quite small changes such as remembering to take medication and being mindful about sleep. However, some make significant changes such as adopting a quieter lifestyle in a rural community and changing jobs. Annie made significant changes.

I am 25 and I was diagnosed with bipolar in 1999. Since then I have had to make huge changes in my life to stay well. Taking medication religiously would be the smallest of these changes. I now lead a different, but full life. I work, have a de facto partner and pets.

I found that stress is a big trigger for my mental health. Managing my mental health, to a large extent, is about managing stress and asking for help. I left a demanding job in the corporate sector, and now work part-time in community health. This means less pressure and more flexibility. I try to ensure that I plan time for holidays and relaxation.

I have worked hard to build up my support networks. I have a great GP. She works closely with my psychiatrist and counsellor. I also made the decision to move closer to my family. It is reassuring to know they are there, if I should need them. The same goes for my friends. My friends all know about my illness and have been incredibly supportive.

Depression is my main form of unwellness. I start to feel irritable, teary and don't want to get out of bed. I may also feel dissociated from other people. I feel that I can't cope and suicide suddenly seems like a viable option. The anxiety will also keep me up at night worrying, heart pounding. I start to feel paranoid that others are going to judge what I say.

The mania is less common. It begins as a pleasant sensation – full of beans, so much to do, let's get out and do it! Others notice that my speech becomes pressured and I have a huge to-do list.

I am now adept at managing signs of mania, but I still struggle daily with anxiety and depression. When I am becoming unwell I find that sharing this experience with a friend or with my psychiatrist is useful. If I am honest with my psychiatrist then he usually offers the level of support and intervention that I need.

My psychiatrist referred me to a counsellor who uses cognitive behavioural therapy. She helps me to combat feelings of anxiety and depression. She is also essential in re-gaining perspective about life's problems. She reminds me that certain life events are stressful for anyone, whether they have bipolar or not.

We also look at my goals and this re-instills hope

when I feel it has gone. This helps prevent a depressive episode. If I am becoming depressed then some gentle exercise is always beneficial. I avoid vigorous aerobic exercise to music, as I find that it can trigger a manic episode.

If I do feel a bit manic then I make myself slow down. I cut down on my daily activities and try and listen to a progressive relaxation tape. I know that if I don't prevent the mania, then I will eventually come crashing down. This is usually enough incentive! So I might tell my partner that I feel a bit manic and he can help by holding me quietly and helping me to restrict my activities.

Many people with manic depression rely on support of partners to help them stay well. People who are single find other resources to rely on. Josephine finds support within her community.

It's pretty drastic but I have chosen to remain single as I haven't yet found a man who could live with someone as exciting as a woman with bipolar illness. Although I am now fifty-three, I am still hopeful.

I have probably had bipolar mental health challenges since I was ten years old. However it took a very long time for me to be diagnosed correctly. Once diagnosed and treated, I have found ways to stay well.

The changes I've made to stay well are primarily to manage stress and pressures in my life and work with a watchful eye. I work closely with my specialist on identifying early signs of undue stress and early symptoms of mood change so I can head them off at the pass with a medication adjustment and lifestyle stress reduction.

I work in a stressful job in health professional service delivery. I find it helpful to see a career counsellor every two months to work through tricky work issues. I also take regular holiday breaks.

I moved to the country for a slower pace of living and to remove myself somewhat from my blood family (whom I love dearly). Being the eldest single daughter, I was often seen as the problem solver.

I regularly see a spiritual director for guidance in my spiritual and prayer life. I also keep a journal to clarify where I and my feelings are at. I have two puppies that I love and who accept me as I am. We all love to walk to the park and on the beach. The restlessness of the ever changing sea seems to be synonymous of life with bipolar.

I also have a small pod of very close 'soul' mates who are my support group, mostly by phone since I have moved to the country. None of them has bipolar illness. I don't keep my illness secret and let people know when I am up or down, without expecting them to heal the situation. I am incredibly gentle on myself and try not to march to anyone else's drum.

No matter what lifestyle people adopt, or where they choose to live, it is not always possible to avoid stress. Tim uses a range of strategies to lessen the impact of his stressful job. These strategies help him to control his illness.

I was diagnosed with manic depression when I was seventeen. For a short time, I was really wired – it was an amazing feeling. I ended up in hospital for about a month. The doctor put me on lithium and I have been taking it ever since. I am now forty-five, and have a masters degree in economics and nearly twenty uninterrupted years working as a stockbroker. It is a frenetic job, but I have learnt to manage the stress. My wife and three children help to keep me grounded.

Even though I consider myself healthy, I still have periods when I wake up in the middle of the night with my thoughts racing. Most often, this is due to some work crisis. I've learnt that waking up at 2 am is not good for me. Lying awake with racing thoughts is one of my warning signs. With my illness, I simply can not afford to take the risk of having too many sleepless nights. So when this happens, I don't hesitate to knock it on the head with a sleeping tablet.

All those self help books tell you to meditate and do yoga, but I'm not that sort of person. I went to a yoga class once and felt like a complete idiot. I hated it. I prefer to take my boat out for a sail, or kick the footy with my son. Maybe I should try meditation. I have spiritual beliefs but I just can't see myself sitting still on a mat. For me, keeping a positive attitude works well enough. Having a positive attitude also helps with my work. I have worked very hard to get where I am. My firm is one of the largest in Melbourne, and I am now one of the bosses.

I use the internet to keep up-to-date with the medical literature. Health care professionals have such a negative view of this illness. They don't seem to think that it is possible for people to control manic depression. Well I can control it, and I am sure others can too. If I control the illness, it doesn't get the chance to control me. It's as simple as that.

Another thing that really bothers me about the medical literature is the assumption that people with manic depression all have low self esteem. Surely, our self esteem has more to do with our parenting than our illness. My parents taught me that I was OK. No illness can ever take that away from me.

Apart from loss of self esteem, the medical literature also describes disrupted relationships, alcoholism and drug abuse, financial chaos, repeat hospitalisations, and unemployment. Clearly, you can't believe everything you read, not even in the medical literature.

I think my decision to quit marijuana made a huge difference to me. When I was a university student, I used to smoke pot a lot. I also used to drink a lot of booze. Now that I am older, I tend to drink less. I prefer a nice glass of wine than to quaff a whole cask.

My GP manages my drugs. I've taken lithium for a long time. It is a bit like brushing my teeth – it is something I remember to do without thinking too much about it. I just need to remember to phone the GP and organize my blood tests every six months or so. My level has been consistently 0.6 for as long as I can remember. These blood tests also monitor my kidneys and thyroid. So far, so good.

My formula for controlling this illness is sleep, prescription drugs, no pot and less grog. All I can say is it has worked for me for most of my adult life. I certainly have not had years consumed by this illness. Despite all the negative stuff you hear about manic depression, I am happily married with kids and a good job.

For some, 'staying well' means being free of symptoms. For others, 'staying well' allows them to make choices and take control of their lives. Nick took control of his life. He wanted to have a job, education, partner, and children. He also wanted to find a trustworthy psychiatrist.

Once I was finally diagnosed and treated correctly, I asked myself what I wanted out of life. I wanted a wife, children of my own, a car, a house . . . in a nutshell, I wanted the better things in life. In order to obtain these things, I needed a job. So I spent the next year or so trying to get a job. After a considerable number of my application letters were rejected, I decided to go back to university so that I could get retrained for work. It took me four years to complete a 3 year degree course. I received no special treatment from the academic staff. I was very proud of my achievement.

During my studies at university, I began to establish a reliable support network around myself. I had decided to choose my own private psychiatrist as the government service treated me with trainees that changed every six months. It took some time, but I now have a doctor whose judgment I trust implicitly. I also began seeing the university's counselling service.

I discovered that I was very good in the field of statistics, the numeric and conceptual realm combined naturally for me. I decided that I wanted to work in this field. While I was still at university, I was head-hunted by a market research company. Most of the work was deadline driven. It entailed periods of high stress. However, by then I was resilient enough to handle it quite well. I also knew the importance of relaxing when the pressure times were over.

Throughout this period I had found that the slow release lithium (priadel) that I was taking helped me to stay well. However a government decision to stop importing priadel had left me with only lithicarb for medication. Given that I am prone to miss the occasional dose, this made my medication regime less reliable. However I was sound enough both physically and emotionally to deal with these things.

I met my partner through a discussion group that I had started for 'well functioning' people with psychiatric disorders. It was known as the 'Bridging Group', and it catered for people who could work full or part time, and were more than adequately handling their disorder. When I started the 'Bridging Group' there was no such place of contact for people who were well.

My partner and I have been together for eight years, and we have a four year old daughter. However the 'Bridging Group' has long since disbanded. During this period of my life my parents were very proud of me. They decided to help me obtain a house. I still live here today with my partner and daughter.

During this period my psychiatrist and I decided to cease my medication. This decision appears to have worked well. On occasions, when my mood appears to be unsettled, he suggests I return to taking lithium.

I accept his judgment until he is satisfied of my stability.

When my daughter was born, I decided to see my doctor on a monthly basis as opposed to the three monthly arrangement we had earlier. I believe there is much more at stake as the breadwinner of this family. I also decided to work part-time.

I have been well now for seventeen years and as time goes on I think less of a coping strategy and more about getting on with life. I do not doubt for a second though that I have bipolar mood disorder, and that my diagnosis is fully accurate, as I have spent much of my youth in turmoil with this condition, and all evidence points to my doctor's diagnosis as being accurate.

Choices

Georgia chose to have three children. When first diagnosed, she thought she would never be able to have children. She had been told about the risks – the heritability of the disorder, risks during pregnancy, and risks during the post-partum period. However, with the support of her husband, family, friends and psychiatrist, she was able to have children. Georgia is glad that her initial fears about having manic depression did not stop her from having children.

When I was first diagnosed with bipolar mood disorder I thought that I would be sick forever. I certainly thought that I would never have children. Before being diagnosed with bipolar, I had several episodes of the illness, one after the other. It was a real rollercoaster ride. Within a few months, I went from being very depressed, then 'out of control' with mania and finally so down that I attempted suicide. What sort of mother would that make me? Besides if I were so mentally ill, I thought I would surely pass the disease on to my children. Nine years later, I am pleased to say that I have my illness 'in hand' and am the proud mother of three young boys – including eighteen-month-old twins.

I needed to plan my pregnancies more carefully than most people, but have had great support from my psychiatrist, my husband, my family and friends. At first I thought I may need to adopt, but after I had stayed well for five years – and felt confident about my ability to cope with having a baby – my husband, psychiatrist and I started to plan for our first child. I had watched my family and friends deal with lack of sleep and extra stresses when they had children. However, I had always wanted children and as I was now in my mid-thirties it was time to 'go for it'!

I could not have attempted having children without the trust I had in my psychiatrist. We had discussed the issue many times, and he had told me about the risks. I was advised to go off my medication before conception. Although I wanted to decrease the risk of foetal abnormalities, I was very nervous about stopping my medication. We were also told that there was a 40% risk of mania or depression during the post-partum period. This seemed very high. However, I was more worried about triggering a relapse from the general stress and sleeplessness of parenting.

My psychiatrist, husband and I worked out a plan

to keep me well both during pregnancy and after the birth. I went off medication to conceive and throughout the pregnancy, which went well. I went straight back on the medication after my baby was born. I also saw the psychiatrist more often during that time. We decided that it would be better for me not to breastfeed because my breast milk may have contained low concentrations of medication. Not breastfeeding also meant that someone else could bottle-feed the baby while I got more sleep. I copped criticism from some of the nurses in the hospital for not even attempting to breastfeed, but then none of them had seen me sick. They didn't really have any understanding of bipolar, which seemed a bit silly considering all the awareness of post-natal depression these days – after all, I was a prime candidate for either post-natal depression or mania! Happily, all the precautions paid off and I was able to really enjoy the first couple of years of motherhood.

As everything went so well with our first child, we decided to try again. Unfortunately, I had a miscarriage which left me feeling very sad. A year or so later, I found I was expecting another baby – except this time around it was twins. It was a difficult pregnancy and the twins were born two months premature, which was very stressful. In hindsight, I think I was complacent about my bipolar. I became so focused on the babies that I forgot about my own health. I was not on medication because I had been managing so well without it. This time I attempted to breastfeed, which meant I was disturbing my sleep, expressing milk at all hours of the day and night. The babies were in special care at the hospital, so I was racing in and out to see them and then back home again to see my toddler. I didn't stop to rest, let alone make an appointment with my psychiatrist. It was a recipe for disaster. After several weeks I ended up in hospital in a state of manic 'overdrive'.

Luckily I did not suffer any depression afterwards, probably because I came to my senses and took action to look after myself properly. I am now back on medication. I check in with my psychiatrist regularly. I have resumed seeing the psychologist I have seen on and off since I was first ill. I have extra help with the kids. My husband shares a lot of the load, so I can get my much needed sleep.

It is a hectic lifestyle, but I am no super-mum, nor can I attempt to be one. I am still learning to take much needed breaks from the children, because I am so set on being a good mother. I have to be quite vigilant not only about sleep and rest, but about monitoring my moods and whether they are 'normal' or not. I'm not really sure what 'normal' is for a woman who has three boys under four, but am aware that I need to manage my stresses. If I don't, I will come 'unstuck'. Like all mothers, with or without a mental illness, I need to look after myself in order to look after my children.

Of course it's still early days, but I have learned a great deal from being sick again. Better still, I have learnt more about how to prevent it. This illness is a lifelong journey – we accumulate knowledge as we travel. I am so glad that my initial fears about my illness did not stop me from having my three gorgeous boys. And if they too suffer from bipolar? Then I of all people will surely be able to help them deal with it.

Health care professionals discuss the risks of pregnancy to couples who wish to have a child.[36] However, Georgia's story shows that, with support, it is possible to stay well as a parent. With careful planning, the stresses can be well managed. It also shows the value of life experience, including episodes of illness, as a learning process.

As a clinical psychologist, Hanna acquired academic knowledge about manic depression. However, her personal life experiences were invaluable in teaching her how to manage her illness responsibly.

It is sometimes difficult for me to know if I am experiencing a normal reaction to a life stress or an episode of illness. Over the years, mania has got me into more trouble than depression.

Although I have a Masters degree in psychology, this only gives me academic insight. There is nothing like the real experience. Sometimes the experts view is far removed from my experience of the illness. My psychiatrist told me that I was 'low level' bipolar. I therefore assumed it would be OK to go off my medications. I went cold turkey. I became very unwell. I will never do that again. Later my psychiatrist told me that I would probably need to stay on tablets for life. He told me that if I took my tablets, I would be able to forget about having the illness. This was the worst advice he could possibly have given me!

I have learnt that I must never ever forget that I have bipolar disorder. It is important that I keep an eye out for warning signs. I have two teenage daughters, so I often have quite a lot of stress in my life. It can't be avoided. So I need to monitor my reactions to stress. I also found menopause a very confusing time. I experienced similar symptoms to bipolar. It was hard to know if it was mania, menopause or just me responding to a stressful event. I needed to be very careful.

It is often necessary for people with manic depression to distinguish between an emotional response to daily life and early warning symptoms of illness. Distinguishing normal moods from mild and moderate expressions of the illness is sometimes an exacting task.[37] However, once people gain insight into themselves and their illness, this task becomes easier.

Most people with manic depression choose to avoid episodes of illness. Wendy recognises when she is becoming unwell. However, she sometimes chooses to enjoy 'moments of mania' in ways that are acceptable to self and others. Her manic moments bring joy and debt, not embarrassment and shame.

The other day, I recognised that I was becoming manic. I love that exhilarating feeling of being high. It is quite addictive. I get this feeling that I can do everything better than anyone. My mind is totally in overdrive. I am clever, funny. I talk too fast. I alliterate. I laugh loudly. I also feel a strong desire to shop. During these moments, I have a choice. I can go straight home, call my psychiatrist, take anti-psychotic medication and sleep for a few days. Alternatively, I can go SHOPPING!

Recently, rather than go home and take medication, I decided to continue shopping. I spent a lot of money buying jewellery. I bought beautiful pieces of jewellery that I would not normally even look at, let alone buy. Every cent was on credit. It was money that I do not have. These moments of mania would be more fun if I was not on the disability pension.

Later that night, I took temazepam and risperdal. I stayed quiet for a few days. Then I phoned my psychiatrist. I told him what had happened and that I was OK. I love my new jewellery, even though I really can't afford it. It will take me a long time to pay it off. But I don't regret it for a moment. I will certainly not be taking it back.

People with manic depression often feel ashamed for inappropriate actions such as financial irregularities.[38] Sometimes people may need assistance to disentangle themselves from financial agreements that were made during 'moments of mania'. Occasionally, however, a manic spending spree may bring pleasure, not pain.

Is this a manic response?

Some people with manic depression worry whenever they feel happy. They are concerned that their feelings of happiness will spill over into an episode of manic euphoria. Others accept that their fast times are when they are most creative. Likewise, they accept a few bad days, knowing that a bad day does not mean they are about to plummet into an episode of depression.

Caroline has gained important insight into herself. She

accepts herself. She also accepts that ups and downs are a normal part of life, not just the illness. She is well aware of signs that indicate that she may be becoming unwell. Caroline has strategies in place to relieve these symptoms.

> I respect and admire the learning and strength that I have gained by having bipolar disorder. I am now able to look at what is a reaction to normal life stress and what is illness. I accept that my fast times are times when I am most creative and have incredible thoughts. I spend time with female friends who are of like mind and spirit. I embrace my exceptional personality instead of focusing on feeling an outcast. I try not to let myself get tired. I say no when I need to. I pray, meditate and have regular massages. I always take my medication.
>
> When things are going wrong, I crave bananas in abundance. I feel over tired, but can't sleep. I wake at three in the morning to think about work, children, money, bills, dog, cat and goldfish! I have exhausting sexual and predator dreams. Energy is like a heavy cloud one-day and the next a hurricane. I think obsessively about something. I have a strong feeling to break 'the rules', shout and dance in public. I get drunk too often. I have excessive restlessness, sometimes anger. I blow out of proportion small things that people say. I start looking for the nearest cliff to jump off!
>
> When I experience my early warning signs, I talk to my specialist. To avoid episodes of illness, I always take my medication. I surround myself with love and affection and channel my creative energy into my

children and work. I let things go that aren't important and stay away from taxing people. I remain organized by setting a time table for myself when things are getting shaky. I make sure I get enough sleep.

It is crucial for people with manic depression to recognise the difference between a typical reaction to an event and reactions that may indicate an imminent episode of illness. Being mindful of manic depression allows people to know when it is necessary for them to intervene with stay well strategies. It also enables people with manic depression to ask for help when they need it. The next chapter looks more closely at those who help – the personal, social and professional networks that enable people with manic depression to stay well.

Chapter 5

Empathy and support

Mental health organisations are 'fighting stigma' by improving community awareness of mental illness and attempting to change people's attitudes. However their 'stop the stigma' campaigns focus predominantly on the negative attitudes in the community towards manic depression. Much less attention is given to the positive attitudes – the kindness and compassion – that are also shown to people with manic depression.

Community

Like many young people, Jason began his journey with manic depression without being diagnosed. As a result, his early adult years were disruptive. After receiving the correct diagnosis, he found support in all kinds of places – flat mates, close friends, case manager, psychiatrist, support group, church choir, books, museums, volunteer work, and writing.

> I was admitted to a psychiatric hospital when I was 17. However, they did not give me a diagnosis at the time. When I was 21, I became quite high as a result of

trying antidepressants, along with other things that were happening. I was attending a university college at the time. I was expelled from college for my unusual and distracting behaviour, something I took as quite a blow as I was enjoying it so much. Soon afterwards my behaviour got worse and I became more manic. I was doing all sorts of stupid things in public with accompanying grandiose delusions. Then I was admitted to hospital. They diagnosed bipolar disorder.

Some time after I got out of hospital I was able to find a new home at my current address. This means that I have been living in the same flat for five years, something I am pleased about. I think having both a stable home where I can afford the rent and people to live with is a great asset. I prefer living with other people because sometimes when I live alone, I become lonely, agitated and restless. For the first three years of living in my flat I attended university doing an Arts degree, which I completed in 2001. Since then I have worked and not worked, in everything from administration to cleaning for a school. So my working life post-uni has been a bit patchy. Just before I finished university, I started receiving the disability support pension.

Despite not working, I have plenty to keep me on the go and I like to think that I live a pretty active and animated social and community life. I have a group of four close friends who I see at least weekly. I go on a walk with one friend each week. We are talking about going to the gym together too which sounds like an effort but should be fun. With this friend I am going to the ballet soon, and we have also been on day trips and gone for walks and lunch. This I really enjoy.

With the trust, responsibility and mutual companionship of this friend (even though he is quite a lot older than me), I have found a solid foundation for life. Finding friends who you like, who like you, who are loyal to you and will not forsake you in whatever circumstance is really a great asset. He feels the ability to tell all his personal problems to me and he knows that I will listen and not judge, not gossip, and give him useful feedback so that he can analyse his life from an objective viewpoint. Of course, I tell him my problems, both new and old, and he provides me with wise counsel and comfort to make decisions about my life with a more enlightened view.

My case manager, who I have been seeing roughly weekly since I got out of hospital five years ago, has been a tremendous support and it is getting to the stage now where we really know and trust each other well. Without him I think I would go crazy, and I do if I don't see him for a couple of weeks or more. My psychiatrist I get on really well with, and although I am just getting to know him, it seems as though it should be a good relationship.

My only regret is that my case is not a little more co-ordinated and that my psychiatrist is not able to spend a solid enough amount of time with me to really know what the problems are and what to do about them. My case manager's advice, although much appreciated, is sometimes too general and non-specialist enough and I don't feel that tabs are being kept on me enough.

Recently I have been attending a bipolar support group which I have found a great help. It meets monthly. Last year, I attended another support group which was good in its own way, and I attended it every week for quite a while.

I have also found great peace from my spiritual journey (even though I am not very religious), and I attend my local church regularly. I also sing in the church choir, which has expanded my horizons into centuries of a rich church choral tradition. I feel that I understand history more through attending church and singing in the choir, something that is important in finding one's place in the world.

Apart from my local church, I also go into St Paul's Cathedral, and St Patrick's Cathedral, Melbourne, for meditation and prayer during the week which I do alone and silently, and I find very spiritually refreshing. I think it greatly enhances the spiritual effect to pray or meditate in beautiful and ancient surroundings and this I find in these cathedrals.

I also do non-Christian spiritual practice. Although I primarily identify with the Christian Church, I am not solely Christian and am open to all faiths. I have recently undertaken a series of sessions in a form of yoga/meditation which is done in a small group and is free. Although I am just starting with this I think it has much to offer and I try to meditate in my home as well.

I have many other interests to keep me occupied. I try to fill most days of my diary with one major activity each day. The activity does not have to be 'big'; it just has to be something. I try not to spend too much time in my house because there is nothing too interesting to do there.

I do very much like to read books particularly art and philosophy books. My love of art, classical and modern, but particularly classical, has led me to visit many art galleries around Melbourne and develop a bit of a collection of my own paintings and pictures at home. I also love museums, and there are a number of different museums in Melbourne which can be viewed at low cost or free. A subject that I did in history at university has led me to a greater cultural and historical awareness of the Melbourne landscape, and I enjoy visiting historic sites and monuments.

I am also involved in politics. I do volunteer work, including handing out how-to-vote-cards at elections. I also have other hobbies, like model-making and writing. I write poetry, short stories and essays. I enjoy showing it to my friends and getting their feedback.

If I think that things are going wrong, I tend to notice that I am getting quite agitated, and talkative. I may want to make contact with others impulsively and make lots of phone calls. With help, I cool down eventually. In crises, I can ring up psychiatric triage which I have done on a few occasions.

Generally speaking, I just ride my periods of minor illness out. They may only last a few hours and generally happen in the evening. If I get agitated at night I can usually trace its source to some form of stress or instability during the day. Having a stable daily routine and a regular bedtime is a must for me. I must avoid getting too excited. This is particularly important at night, so for this reason I do not do much late night partying.

Depression is very unpleasant, and can feed on itself to do long-lasting damage. However, it can be treated with the right dose of antidepressant. It also helps when a few things go right. Just doing something that makes me happy often helps. I read a book on happiness once – there is a great deal of self-help literature out there.

Mania, I think, is more dangerous than depression assuming that the depression is not suicidal. Therefore, it is more important to watch out for yourself when you are high than when you are low. When you are high, you can do lasting damage to your name and reputation, but when you are low it just feels bad. I wear out the bad times and know that soon I will be happy again.

Jason stays well by staying busy within a friendly community. Although he does not undertake paid employment, he maintains a regular routine with a range of social, spiritual and sporting activities. He also finds enjoyment and fulfillment in voluntary activities. To avoid problems, he seeks counsel from friends, professionals and self help books. Each plays a helpful role in Jason's stay well plan.

Family

With the assistance of her husband, children and psychiatrist, Diana is able to respond early to her warning signals. With education and experience, her family learnt to recognise changes in her behaviour, mood and energy. Their compassionate support helps her to have a happy and productive life.

I am living proof that it is possible to lead a normal life with full quality once the illness is diagnosed and controlled. I have a wonderful quality of life and live life to the full. On looking back on my life of fifty-nine years I can actually say I would prefer to be allotted manic depression once diagnosed and 'controlled' than some other insidious physical illness. It is not my enemy as I originally thought. I have grown to understand that the illness consists of deep mood swings. With medication, these mood swings are much shallower. This enables everyday life to go on.

I first became ill at the age of 30, three months after the death of my father. I had two young daughters. I was very concerned about the effect of my illness on them. I adored them, and still do. Luckily, my wonderful husband was there to support me.

With the illness, I had feelings of massive panic. I would break down in tears all the time, so I did not want to see people. I would also wake in the morning and think, 'Oh no, not another day'. I felt sheer terror and panic. After appointments with many different GPs and specialists, I finally reached a psychiatrist who explained I was experiencing depression with a high level of anxiety. He diagnosed manic depression. No more fighting to know what was wrong with me – what a relief!

For two years, I was treated with psychological therapy. After that, I started medication with lithium and epilim. I was also prescribed an anti-depressant, as my mood swings are more often depression than mania. With mania I do excessive shopping. I have learnt to lay-by so I can cancel any big buys. Although I fought against taking lithium, I am convinced that it is a wonder-drug. Since taking lithium, my lows and highs are much less extreme. My friends and acquaintances all advised me not to take it. Eventually, I chose to take it. I have learnt that bipolar is due to a chemical imbalance. It is an actual illness that can happen to anyone.

My husband and I have brought up two wonderful daughters plus a surrogate daughter. We are very close to them. We have two great son-in-laws and now a granddaughter and grandson who I look after regularly each week. We also have dogs and cats. I also have many friends, including some close ones.

When our children were young, we lost all our money in our business. We had to sell our house. This would cause great stress for anyone, with or without this illness. Yet I coped. I quickly learnt the electric typewriter and I took a secretarial job. I stayed there for ten years for the children's education.

I now have insight into my feelings and my body and can feel when a mood swing is imminent. These days, with lithium and my other medications, I never swing down for long. So I have no fear of the highs and depths. When I start to spend money, I may be heading for a high; when I start to lose my self-esteem, I may be heading for a low. On feeling a mood swing coming, I talk with my family. It helps me enormously to know that they understand and support me.

If my mood slides, I contact my psychiatrist. After assessing me, he invariably adjusts my medication. This in itself gives me confidence to push on knowing I will be OK soon. Other things that help me to manage my mood swings are yoga and meditation.

Meditation helps very much when stressed or depressed. I also find that exercise helps me to feel calmer.

What I really want to do is give hope to others still learning to control their own bipolar illness. The illness has done so much good for my life and my family. Rather than be weighed down by me or my experience of illness, my children have benefited. They have grown up with so much insight and compassion. They treat bipolar as a normal illness and have never felt any shame in telling their friends about my illness.

In a joint effort of my wonderful husband, family and specialist over the last twenty-nine years I have led a very fulfilling rewarding happy and insightful life. The main thing I ever wanted to achieve in life was to be a good wife and loving mum. I feel I achieved this by coming to understand my response to bipolar like the back of my hand. With insight, my family and I have been able to move swiftly to intercept a mood swing.

Close friends and family are often in a unique position to observe changes in behaviour and moods. It is often beneficial for close friends and family members to also receive education about manic depression. Education can provide important insights to help them to recognise early warning signs. By learning to recognise early warning signs, close friends and family are able to help people with manic depression to intervene early.

Health care professionals often educate close friends and family to watch for expansiveness and undue enthusiasm, involvement in excessive numbers of projects, changes in sexual and financial behaviour, poor judgment. However, these are all late signs of an impending episode of mania. It is more helpful to educate partners, close friends and family to recognise early, not late, warning signs. In particular, they need to be aware of the subtle changes in behaviour that may indicate that all is not well. Often only people with manic depression, and people close to them, will notice these subtle changes in behaviour. Partners, close friends and family can be taught various ways to respond to these early warning signs.

Talking about behavioural changes and early warning signs with a person with manic depression can be extremely helpful. It is often reassuring to have someone to check behaviour, particularly when a person with manic depression is speeding up. However, sometimes such surveillance is oppressive. Louisa felt her behaviour was being constantly monitored.

For years, I have had to stay calm around my older brothers. They are both doctors – the type who think they know everything about everything. Ever since I was first diagnosed – when I was a teenager – I have felt them looking at me for signs of illness. Whenever I argue with them about politics, they ask me whether I am still taking my tablets. I can't even laugh without feeling their eyes on me. It is so annoying. Nowadays, I don't even try to share my views, or humour, with them.

A few years ago, we had a terrible Christmas. One of my sister-in-laws launched a vitriolic attack on my family. I was tempted to ask her if she had remembered to take her lithium, but felt my joke would probably not amuse anyone but me. Instead, I went home and wrote a story about her. My short story grew into an epic about my entire family. I was rather proud of it. So I sent copies to all my siblings. Some loved it, but my eldest brother immediately diagnosed mania. The writing was too heart-felt – I must be bonkers. He even showed my family story to a psychiatrist. To make matters more ludicrous, my brother threatened to sue me if I ever published the story.

I was so shocked and angry that I stopped sleeping. After two nights of not sleeping, I recognised that I was becoming unwell. I went to a 24 hour clinic and got some sleeping tablets. My intention was to come home and spend a few days sleeping it off. My brother, however, soon put a stop to that. Rather than contact my local doctor, he contacted the cavalry. The Crisis Assessment and Treatment Team were at my door when I arrived home from the clinic and it was all downhill from there.

A psychologist and a psychiatric nurse came to my home and, after a brief assessment, they recommended that I take a major tranquilliser. I refused to take the medication and angrily insisted that they leave my home. Soon afterwards, they returned with the police and I was forcibly removed from my home. I was transferred to hospital in the back of a police divisional van.

There are occasions when family and friends may need to intervene on behalf of someone with manic depression. In these situations, it is important to have an advanced directive that all parties – the person with manic depression, their partner, family, friends and health care professionals – have agreed upon. A 'crisis management plan' helps people with manic depression to feel assured that their wishes will be respected. It also helps family and friends to feel comfortable with their interventions. A 'crisis intervention plan' provides people with manic depression the opportunity to regain some control over any future interventions. It also provides some peace of mind.

Professional therapy

When Vicky was at her most vulnerable, she required professionals working in the mental health system to show her respect and compassion. However, being transported to hospital in a police divisional van is an example of punitive, not compassionate, treatment.

> During an episode of mania, I was forcibly removed from my home by the police (like a criminal) and locked in a very small cell (like a criminal). The inhumanity towards me in the psychiatric hospital was disgraceful. There is one memory of hospital that stands out: the heavily medicated patients lying around, some on couches, some on the floor, while the nursing staff sat in the office observing through a glass window. A few of us paced up and down a corridor, forty four paces in each direction. There was nothing else to do; it was either the couch or the corridor.
>
> People treat their pets with more compassion than I was shown in hospital. Yet my letter to the chief psychiatrist, outlining my experiences in hospital, was

dismissed. In his eyes, the label of 'manic-depressive' removed my credibility and silenced my testimony.

The first thing I needed to do when I was discharged from hospital was to apologise to those people who had been affected by my manic behaviour. This apology was a very important part in my recovery process. I felt very remorseful and ashamed for my irresponsible behaviour when I was sick and I hoped for forgiveness.

I rang my neighbour who had been with me when I was sick. Upon hearing my voice, she hung up the phone. I was devastated. Several weeks later, I wrote an apology letter, but it was returned to me unopened. At a time when I desperately needed compassion, I found hostility. Losing my neighbour's friendship due to my behaviour when I was sick has caused me sadness – much more sadness than the illness itself.

Although it often takes only a few weeks to recover from the illness itself, the 'side effects' of the treatment can take much longer to resolve. Some people with manic depression never forget the inhumane treatment they received in hospital. Others, like Terry, are able to move on. With a dual diagnosis of manic depression and HIV, he experienced some health care professionals who demonstrated discriminatory attitudes. However, Terry also remembers the kindness that was shown to him.

Suffering from a mental illness can often be a very lonely, complicated and often tortured existence, but not for me. At 25, I have now learnt to manage my condition in many various ways. I also receive a lot of support from a great psychiatric support team, amazingly honest friends, a great family and the best lover in the world.

I was first hospitalized for a suicide attempt when I was 12 years old. I was admitted to the Royal Children's Hospital where my treatment was inappropriate for a young adolescent. There was no psychiatric unit at the time and I was put in a ward with infants. I was treated meanly by the nurses – I was reprimanded and scolded for trying to kill myself. They told me to snap out of what I was feeling. It was a big ordeal to deal with my family, school and friends, let alone having to deal with negative attitudes from the nurses as well. I was then transferred to an adolescent unit where I met some amazing people who helped me a lot.

Since my first hospitalisation, I have been admitted to various psychiatric hospitals around Melbourne. Without medication, I used to become manic and uncontrollable. I had to be admitted for the safety of myself and my loved ones. I am now on medication and have been for five years. If I stay on the medication and keep up with my therapy, I am sure that I can quite easily live a normal life. Normal to me is being free and able to make positive life choices that do not harm other people.

I think my illness was so severe because I was punished for being a young queer man. Health care professionals used to abuse me, emotionally and psychologically. I wore my sexuality on my sleeve – I am proud to be gay. A social worker once said to me: 'I don't like you and I don't like your lifestyle. We are going to do everything in our power to stop you from living with that man'. To me, this was a direct form of homophobia. A lot of social workers at that office hated me because I wasn't 'a good little boy'. They also hated me because I did not play by their rules.

I grew up quick, lived on the street and was a sex worker at the age of 13. So what? Big deal – I did what I could to survive. Back then, there were a lot of negative people working in all the government departments. They should not have been there – they were not qualified and had no life experience to deal with gay issues or people with mental illness.

In contrast, people working at the hostel were the nicest and most open minded people. They gave me and my partner a lot of hope. They gave us nothing but respect and love. They encouraged me to seek help with my problems. I did not want to get the social workers involved as they did not know how to deal with me at all.

Due to so many bad experiences during my adolescence, I decided to create a new person. I created my alter ego and my drag queen persona, Alo Vera. This bubbly character is a happy person who is always trying to please people. When I put on a frock, I feel empowered and ready to cope with anything. My alter ego is a safe sex crusader. She believes in sexual freedom and complete honesty when you meet new casual partners. She is an HIV/AIDS activist. Yes, I just happen to be HIV positive.

Being Alo Vera helps me to cope with both my illnesses. I am able to reach out to people at night clubs – even total strangers – talking, touching, laughing, and having a beer or an ecstasy or two. It is when people take ecstasy and other party enhancers – at raves, clubs, restaurants, parties or friends' houses – that underlying and powerful emotions come to the surface. Sometimes ecstasy gives me a little escape from living with manic depression – I enter a funny, enchanting, romantic and wonderful world. Sometimes, even when I have not taken ecstasy, I feel so happy for no reason. This is not mania, it is pure happiness.

The person who is so special to me is my life partner. I would not be alive today without him. We met when I was 13 and I moved in with him when I was 14, with my mother's consent. We are still together despite all the hatred and loathing we faced from the government welfare organisations, the courts, the police and even some people within our own queer community because of our age difference. This man is my rock, lover, carer and the one person in this world I can depend upon besides myself. If a queer marriage was legal in this country I know we'd be at the altar in a shot (but I guess he'd have to first divorce his wife). In the past, when I was in hospital for manic episodes, he visited me every day. When I was diagnosed with HIV, he was there to support me. He has shown me so much love and kindness. I love this man so much, yet when I was unwell, I hurt him. Now, I go to anger management classes, keep my appointments with my case manager, psychotherapist, psychiatrist and the rest of my support team. We are also having relationship counselling for HIV positive couples. I am doing my best to manage my dual diagnoses.

When professionals refer to 'dual diagnosis', they are commonly referring to mental illness and substance abuse.[39]

However, it is not only alcohol and drugs that impact on the symptoms of manic depression. Many physical illnesses, and their treatments, can exacerbate symptoms of manic depression.

Support groups

There is now a growing awareness of the benefits of support groups for people with manic depression. For some, support groups are an ongoing source of camaraderie and information about the illness, medication and other treatments. It is also a place to share personal stories about experiences of living with manic depression. Support groups helped Norma to be more confident.

> I was one of the original members of the mood support groups. These groups opened new horizons and opportunities for me. My involvement in these groups gave me more self esteem. I became more mature because I was learning to accept, understand and control my life. These groups helped me to feel confident. I thought about my life. I began to manage my home much better. I was happy to garden and felt more enthusiastic about housework.
>
> I think the secret to my recovery was the experience of being with other sufferers. They helped me to trust, to hope and know that you were not alone. They helped me to be more down to earth and cope with reality. I grew stronger. My consumer friends encouraged and counselled me.
>
> Group therapy is still so beneficial and healing for

me. The mood support group provides therapy through their art, writing and social activities. It also keeps me up to date with talks, discussions and the latest literature.

Health care professionals are generally in favour of people with manic depression attending support groups. In a US survey of people who attended 'bipolar support groups', 95% stated that their participation in support groups helped them in communicating with their doctor, being motivated to follow medical instructions, and being willing to take medication.[40] Although support groups may help people with manic depression to comply with medical treatments, they can also give people the confidence to challenge medical treatments.

Paul attended a support group when he was first diagnosed with manic depression. He is concerned for the well-being of people who continue to attend support groups after their 'use-by-date' has expired.

After my first episode of mania, it was important for me to be with people with whom I could laugh at my craziness, rather than feel shame and embarrassment. Fortunately, some old school friends helped me to find some humour in it all. They certainly helped me to get over the post episode hump. I also found the support group very helpful. I needed contact with people who had experienced an illness like mine and recovered from it.

After my discharge from hospital, I was afraid that I would be disabled for the rest of my life. Some people in the support group gave me hope that I would get back to my normal life. However, it was also a big shock to see others who were so disabled by the illness. It made me realise that this illness has an enormous spectrum – some people, like me, experience short episodes of illness; others experience huge disability.

Some people in the support group had been coming to meetings for years, long after the support group's use-by-date had expired. Each month they came, drank coffee, smoked, and talked about the illness, drug reactions, and problems with Centrelink. It seemed that living with the illness had become their entire life. Maybe it would have been better for them to join a sporting club or something.

One of the secrets for me getting back on my feet was getting back to work. At first I did some voluntary work, and then went back to work as a builder. I was quite keen to continue some mental health advocacy work, but the sessions are always scheduled during the day-time. I think people who run these mental health organisations assume that everyone with bipolar is unemployed and on the disability pension. If they opened their eyes and looked outside the mental health system, they may see many of us with manic depression are ordinary people, just like them.

Within hospitals, community health centres and mental health organisations, boundaries are often created between 'us' – the sick person – and 'them' – the competent professional. A few years ago, a mental health organisation used the slogan 'We Help You To Help Them'. The slogan was catchy, but the underlying assumptions were misguided. Their slogan assumed a distinction between 'us' and 'them'. Kay Jamison is one person who publicly blurs the boundaries – she is both 'us' (person with manic depression) and 'them' (Professor of Psychiatry). Her decision to disclose her illness has helped numerous people from all around the world. However, several medical colleagues felt it would have been 'best' to keep her illness private.[41] Best for whom?

Staying well at work

People with manic depression develop strategies to manage their work lives, including workplace stress. These strategies may include part-time work, regular holidays, or even weekly shiatsu massages. However, these personal strategies work best when there is also a sensitive and aware work environment.

People with manic depression use their own judgment when deciding whether to disclose personal information to colleagues at work. Andrea decided to tell her boss that she had manic depression. She did not expect him to announce it to all her colleagues during a staff meeting.

> After my breakdown, I anticipated that returning to work would be uncomplicated. I was wrong. Whilst I had been away on sick leave, my boss had taken it upon himself to tell all my colleagues about my breakdown – he announced 'the breakdown' at a staff meeting. He also met with specific colleagues in my section to find out whether my manic behaviour had upset them in any way. I wonder what he would do if

I had herpes. Would he interview all the staff to see who had shared my coffee mug?

During these extraordinary interviews, some colleagues used the lens of a mental illness to re-interpret my behaviour and their relationship with me. They complained that I was 'direct, honest, articulate and outspoken' (it's true, I am). My boss used these qualities as evidence of my madness.

I had no choice but to resign from work. Being unemployed made my recovery harder. But I could not have stayed working in such a hostile environment. It only took a couple of months to find another job. I've been employed here for about eight years. This time, I keep my illness quiet. What they don't know can't hurt me.

After an episode of illness, an understanding and supportive workplace can assist a person in their transition back to daily life. In the next story, an engineer stays well at work by disclosing his illness. Although Jim encounters some discrimination at work, he also has a compassionate colleague to help him monitor his moods and behaviour at work.

I've had manic depression for thirty years. I had a full working life as an electrical engineer. After my diagnosis became known at work, my career progression slowed down. It was probably discrimination, but there were also benefits. I was able to work in a less stressful position. Most people at work were pretty good, but there was one colleague who always dismissed my ideas because of my manic depression.

I have made many changes in my life. These have not been made just on the basis of my mental health, but it was certainly a consideration. Rather than move back to the stresses of city life, I chose to stay living in a rural area. I was working in a supportive workplace. There was an older person at work who I respected and would listen to. He didn't let me get too high. He would say to me 'You need a break' or 'You're racing too much'. That worked well for me whilst I worked in the country. When I returned to the city, I had to be more careful. Some colleagues react unfavorably to my passion.

I get quite upset easily when things are not done properly at work. I often express this in a way people interpret as anger. Sometimes, I see fear in their eyes. I feel I should be able to get angry when people give me sloppy work. After all, it is their problem, not mine. They seem to think that I am about to lose it and go off the rails. It is better if I just stay low key. I don't let myself become too passionate, not even about footy tipping.

The next story is about prejudice in the workplace. Joanne found it difficult to disclose her personal vulnerabilities to her work colleagues.

I was diagnosed with bipolar disorder during my final year of nursing training. I really believe that having bipolar has enriched my life as a nurse. My empathy towards all patients altered. The experience of being vulnerable made me a more compassionate nurse.

I talk openly about my illness. I consider it my community service to educate people around me. I talk about it everywhere – except work. I have never felt safe to tell my medical and nursing colleagues. Doctors and nurses say some pretty awful things about 'nutters' and 'loonies'. It would be very hard for me to turn around and say I am one of them.

I went back to university in my late 30s and then got a job as a lecturer in a school of social work. I assumed people at university would be educated, so I chose to tell the head of school that I had manic depression. In reply, he told me that he had bunions. If only his attitudes were representative of the rest of the staff.

The first glimpse of my colleagues' prejudice occurred at a faculty planning day. A senior academic colleague used a photograph of Luna Park to represent his workplace – he called the psychiatric hospital a 'funny farm'. Most colleagues laughed. However, those of us who had experienced the mental health system were speechless.

The second hiccup occurred soon after when a lecturer came into the tea room at lunch time – she was distressed because a student had confided that he had a mental illness. She was afraid he might 'go bonkers' and upset the other students. She wanted the student removed from her class. She also wanted to terminate his candidature – she felt that 'these sorts of people' can not work as social workers.

I probably should have spoken up and told her that I had nursed for twenty years with manic depression, but her strong prejudices made this extremely difficult. Instead I simply asked her whether she had been given permission to disclose the student's illness to all of us in the tea room. She replied that she did not need his permission. She felt it was imperative that we were aware of his mental illness so we can 'keep a watchful eye out for his behaviour'.

Professionals disagree about whether students with manic depression should be allowed to study courses such as medicine, nursing and social work. Some believe that an intimate understanding of the illness is beneficial.[42] Others believe that health care professionals with manic depression will disrupt health care services, no matter how well their illness is managed.[43] With such attitudes, it is not surprising that Nikki prefers to keep quiet about her illness.

I am a social worker, as well as a wife and mother. I used to tell people at work that I have bipolar disorder. But not anymore. I am treated much more respectfully in my new job. No-one here knows that I have bipolar disorder.

In my old job, I was often quite anxious. Public hospitals are stressful environments. I used to get too involved with clients' problems. I wanted to fix everything. I also used to be very impatient and intolerant of my managers. It is not a good idea for someone with bipolar to get angry with their managers. One day, I was angry because the senior manager came to a meeting without having done the required background reading. He wanted me to 'talk him through' the documents. I told him that the meeting was a waste of time. I also accused him of wasting the taxpayer's money. In response, he asked me if I was still taking my anti-psychotic medication. This comment shocked me. I had told him about my illness in confidence. He had abused my trust by disclosing my illness to my colleagues.

Soon after this experience, I moved to my current workplace. This time, I decided to keep my illness quiet. I was not going to be publicly humiliated again.

People often blame their illness for the way they behave. Not me. My illness was not responsible for my temper tantrums at work. I was responsible. When I started this new job, I decided to see an anger management counsellor. I also decided to have weekly massages.

The counsellor taught me to be clear about what is important, and what's not. Staying well is important – not just for me, but also for my sons. I now work three days a week and take holidays every six months. Part-time work gives me extra time to spend on things that I really enjoy. I have gone back to university to study social theory. I enjoy spending time in the university library reading and thinking.

I now avoid people who are emotionally draining. I have also finally learnt to let trivial conflict go. I prefer conciliation rather than conflict. I also have a magnificent vegetable garden. Digging the garden is more worthwhile than getting angry at thoughtless managers.

Even in supportive workplaces, stress at work can make people with manic depression vulnerable to an episode of illness. Developing personal strategies to manage work, and minimise stress, helps people with manic depression to stay well at work.

The next chapter brings together the common themes that help people with manic depression to stay well. It concludes with some examples of stay well plans. The stay well plans are not prescriptive plans. They merely contain some examples of what works for some people. It may, or may not, work for others.

Chapter 6

Staying well with a stay well plan

There are no tricks, secrets or special hand shakes required for people with manic depression to stay well. People learn (often through trial and error) what works for them, and what does not work. For some, controlling manic depression involves major lifestyle changes. These changes may include moving out of the city, adopting a quieter lifestyle, and changing jobs. For others, it may be as simple as getting enough sleep.

This chapter brings together the diverse stay well plans that have been described throughout the book. Although there is not a 'one-fix-fixes all' approach to staying well with manic depression, there are some common themes. For many, controlling manic depression involves:

- acceptance
- knowledge
- adequate amounts of sleep
- manageable levels of stress (at both work and play)
- lifestyle (exercise, diet)
- insight into what triggers the illness
- awareness of warning signs
- interventions to deal with warning signs
- suitable medication and other therapies
- supportive workplaces

- compassionate communities and social support networks
- reliable and trustworthy professional support

Stay well themes

Acceptance

For many, the first step to wellness is to be given the correct diagnosis. The next step is to accept the diagnosis. When people accept their illness, and learn about it, they are often able to take more control of their lives.

Knowledge

Staying well involves learning about manic depression. It also involves gaining self knowledge. An important source of knowledge about self and manic depression is life experience, including episodes of illness. With time and experience, people can develop the wisdom to manage their illness and stay well.

Sleep

Sleep is a crucial ingredient to staying well. Rather than lie awake at night, buzzing with ideas or thinking about something stressful, it is often healthier to take a sleeping tablet.

Managing stress

It is not always possible to avoid stress. It is, however, possible to develop strategies to minimise the impact of stress. People have various ways to wind down. Strategies may include regular holidays, shiatsu massages, yoga, meditation, exercise, counselling, friends and so on. These 'wind down' strategies may not always work. It may be necessary to alter medication during particularly stressful periods.

Lifestyle

People with manic depression benefit from eating healthy foods (and avoiding too much junk), exercising, drinking less alcohol/caffeine, spending time with loved ones, avoiding negativity, having quiet times, managing stress, laughing and so on. We all do. However, there are times when these activities are much easier said than done. When feeling down, it may be difficult to exercise – people who are feeling down often just want to lie around, eat junk food and maybe drink alcohol. A stay well plan can prevent people becoming more depressed.

Awareness

It is important to be aware of triggers and mood states. With awareness, it is possible to stay in control of the situation by implementing stay well strategies. For example, when speeding up, people often minimize external stimulation, take long quiet walks, eat healthy foods and, most importantly, have long sleeps.

Insight

A number of factors may trigger an episode of manic depression. These include fatigue, jet lag, hormonal fluctuations, change of seasons, all night partying and recreational drugs. The most common triggers are stress and sleep deprivation. The relationship between these two triggers is complex. In some cases stress causes disruption to sleep. In other cases, a lack of sleep causes a low resilience to stress. Either way, people with manic depression are quick to implement their stay well interventions.

Interventions
Stay well interventions may involve cancelling a few social engagements, getting a few good sleeps, meditation, increasing medication, yoga or making an appointment with a health care professional. With experience, people learn how to respond to warning signals to ensure they avoid episodes of illness.

Medication
Although staying well is rarely just about taking prescribed medication, medication is an important component of many stay well plans. To be more precise, the right medication at the right dose. Most contributors take their medication without fail – no ifs, buts, even when feeling good. They also have regular blood tests.

Social support
Partners, parents, children, brothers, sisters, friends and colleagues gain insight into manic depression. This 'outside insight' often helps people with manic depression to manage their illness. When loved ones ask 'are you OK?' people with manic depression are invited to reflect on their mood. 'Outside insight' is often welcomed.

Professional support
People with manic depression benefit from relationships with professionals that are based on mutual respect. However, the quality of professional psychiatric support varies enormously. It is often worth shopping around for the most suitable health care professionals.

Stay well plans

Stay well plans are strategies that people use to stay well. Many of the strategies are everyday strategies. We all try to avoid conflict at work, exercise, eat properly and sleep well. However, the stakes are often higher for people with manic depression. For example, a couple of sleepless nights will make most people feel very tired, even exhausted. In contrast, a couple of sleepless night may tip a person with manic depression into an acute episode of illness.

Stay well plans are often developed with others – partners, family, close friends, and health care professionals. These stay well plans may be a verbal agreement or an informal written document that is shared with others. Having a documented stay well plan helps people with manic depression to clearly identify their triggers and warning signs. It also allows people to share their stay well strategies with others. This helps partners, family and friends to feel comfortable with any intervention that may be required.

In the following section, four stay well plans have been developed from an amalgam of contributors' strategies. These examples illustrate different types of stay well plans in various life situations. Although these stay well plans may appear rigid, they can be adapted and revised as required. They demonstrate how people use their own life experiences and circumstances to develop unique stay well plans. From these examples, others with manic depression will be able to create their own stay well plans.

Examples of stay well plans

Rob is a 40 year old merchant banker. His job requires frequent overseas travel between offices in London, New York and Melbourne. His first episode of mania occurred soon after flying home from New York. After this, Rob developed a stay well plan to avoid 'jet lag mania'. In addition, Rob developed a stay well plan for those times when he needs to work late at night. Finally, Rob needed strategies to cope with the change of seasons.

* * *

ROB'S STAY WELL PLAN

My main triggers:

1. Jet lag
2. Change of seasons
3. Increased work demands

My warning signs:

1. Obsess about a work problem or idea
2. Talk faster than usual
3. Feel a sense of urgency
4. Difficulty completing tasks
5. Wake up in the middle of night thinking about work problem or idea

Strategies for travelling overseas:

1. In addition to my regular epilim, I always travel with sleeping tablets and anti-psychotic medication, just in case.
2. Always take a temazepam to help me sleep on the plane.
3. Monitor my mood upon arrival.

4. Check in to my hotel and sleep for a few hours, even if day-time.
5. Travel with time to spare.
6. If wide awake in the middle of the night, do not hesitate to take my sleeping and anti-psychotic medication.
7. Always take out travel medical insurance.

Strategies during peak work times:
1. Be aware of my limits.
2. Ensure a good night's sleep by taking additional, preventative medication, as recommended by my psychiatrist.
3. Keep regular 'mood checks' with partner, watching for signs that I may be a bit high (e.g. talking faster than usual, difficulty concentrating on tasks).
4. If partner and/or work colleagues notice any behavioural changes (e.g. speaking faster than usual), listen to them.
5. If speeding up, turn off my computer and go for a jog/swim then take a long bath.
6. If continue to speed up take anti-psychotic medication and contact my psychiatrist.
7. Remember that my health is more important than my work.
8. Take some time off in lieu of the extra work hours.

Strategies during spring:
1. Schedule my annual holidays in spring.
2. Remain aware of the impact that the change of season is having on me.
3. Listen to my partner, particularly if she thinks I am speeding up.
4. If I exhibit hypomanic behaviour, contact my psychiatrist.

Susie is a 32 year old high school teacher. She recently started living with her boyfriend. Recently, her parents have been in the process of an acrimonious divorce. This has made her family life extremely stressful.

* * *

SUSIE'S STAY WELL PLAN

Main triggers:
1. Family stress
2. Coffee – caffeine can interfere with my sleep

Warning signs:
1. Buy more than one Tattslotto ticket
2. Visit adult book shops
3. Writing late at night

To prevent spending excessive amounts of money, I will:
1. Open 2 separate bank accounts, with only one linked to automatic teller machines.
2. Keep a maximum of $200 in the account linked to automatic teller machines.
3. Shop with cash only – no credit cards.
4. Use lay-by facilities.
5. When I feel a desire to gamble (e.g. buy Tattslotto tickets), contact my gambling anonymous support group.

To ensure a good night's sleep, I will:
1. Not drink coffee after 4 pm.
2. Turn my computer off between 6 pm and 6 am.
3. Exercise after work.
4. Drink a maximum of 2 glasses of wine with dinner.
5. Avoid intellectual stimulation after 10 pm on a week night.

6. Keep weekly appointment with counsellor – to discuss family issues
7. Avoid all night partying.
8. Take a sleeping tablet if wake up in the middle of the night, or unable to go to sleep.

To avoid sexual indiscretions, I will:
1. Monitor my moods.
2. Take lithium religiously.
3. Discuss any increase in my sex drive with my boyfriend.
4. Have sex with myself as required.
5. Never go to night clubs on my own.
6. Avoid excessive sexual stimuli (e.g. adult book shops).

Jodie is a 28 year old single mother who has taken twelve months maternity leave from her job as a legal secretary. With a new baby boy (Sam), sleep and rest are crucial. Her stay well plan includes the help of family and friends. A baby who is bottle fed is able to sleep at her sister's house one night per week. This allows Jodie to have some uninterrupted sleep. If she requires additional help, family and friends are only a phone call away.

* * *

JODIE'S STAY WELL PLAN

Main triggers:
1. Parenting (exhaustion and sleep deprivation).
2. Hormonal changes.

Warning signs:
1. No interest in socialising with friends.
2. Sensitive about mothering skills.

3. Irritable with Sam.
4. Teary during the nightly news.
5. Not keeping up with washing, cooking and cleaning.
6. Buying take away food more often than usual.

To stay well, I must:

1. Use formula to feed Sam, not breast milk.
2. Re-commence lithium.
3. Remember to keep scripts and blood tests up-to-date.
4. Keep a regular routine for both myself and Sam.
5. Take Sam to my parent's every Monday and Friday.
6. Take Sam to sister's on Wednesday nights.
7. Go to the gym with a girlfriend on Mondays and Friday mornings. Spend the rest of the day doing restful and enjoyable activities.
8. Become actively involved in local mothers group.
9. Keep the fridge stocked with healthy food by going to the local food and vegetable market with my brother every Saturday morning.
10. Arrange at least one friend to visit each week (and accept offers to bring food when visiting).
12. Touch base with my best friend each evening – either quick SMS, email or short phone call.
12. Enforce strict sleep times for both myself and Sam.
13. Keep regular monthly appointments with psychiatrist, and phone her if I have any concerns.
14. Not watch TV news.
15. If Sam cries all night or is sick, seek help from family, friends or maternal and child health nurse.

Peter is a 50 year old single man who works as a GP in a small country town. He experienced his first episode of mania while working night shift as a resident in a busy hospital emergency department. This was followed by a long episode of depression. For many years, he remained undiagnosed and untreated. His previous wife enjoyed his mood swings, particularly his highs. In his mid-40s, he finally sought help from a psychiatrist. He commenced lithium. Soon after, he moved to the country for a change of pace. His wife did not come with him. Now that he was treated, her role in his life had changed. He has developed a stay well plan which includes the help of his neighbour. He stays in touch with his city psychiatrist by phone.

* * *

PETER'S STAY WELL PLAN

Main triggers:

1. Anger
2. Shift work

Warning signs:

1. No energy or desire to get out of bed in the morning.
2. Low self esteem.
3. Unable to concentrate at work.

To stay well, I must:

1. Keep regular times to go into, and get out of, bed
2. Schedule a one hour lunch break and take a walk around the lake.
3. Attend yoga and meditation classes every week.
4. Talk to my psychologist when things are troubling me either at work or home.

5. Take dietary supplements as recommended by my naturopath.
6. Take short holidays every six months.
7. Say 'no' when someone wants me to do something that will cause me to rush.
8. Listen to my fridge magnet which says 'A dog-walk a day will keep the doctor away'.
9. Keep stimulated, but not over stimulated.
10. Take time out to practise my bass guitar.
11. Stay in touch with family and friends.
12. Attend Tuesday night band practice.
13. Never again accept a job that requires shift work.

When beginning to feel down, I must:

1. Phone my neighbour and arrange to walk with him and our dogs for 45 minutes each morning before work.
2. Stock mostly healthy food in the fridge.
3. Take a sleeping tablet if not asleep by 2 am.
4. If 3 nights of disrupted sleeping, phone psychiatrist.
5. Allow my neighbour to phone my psychiatrist on my behalf (if I am unwilling to make the phone call myself).

CONCLUSION

This book has provided a wellness view of manic depression. Although the stay well stories and plans do not represent all people who experience manic depression, these stories fill an important gap in our understanding of manic depression. Rather than focus only on the 'burden' of manic depression, it is crucial to also listen to people who stay well. These stories provide proof that people with manic depression can aspire to full lives.

Stories in this book may provide hope for other people with manic depression, their families and friends. They may also provide important new insights for health care professionals. According to health care professionals, people with manic depression can, at best, aspire to 'a relatively normal life'.[44] However, people with manic depression do not aspire to live a 'relatively normal life'. We aspire to so much more.

With a competent therapist, the correct diagnosis and up-to-date information about manic depression, people are able to move on with their lives. By learning what works for them, and what does not work, people can actively manage manic depression. Like others who experience chronic illness, people are able to take control of their lives and stay well.

People with manic depression develop strategies to manage their illness. Many people describe the importance of being mindful that they have manic depression. Although people with manic depression would undoubtedly like to forget about their illness, they benefit from maintaining an awareness of its presence. By keeping manic depression in mind, people can learn how to stay well.

REFERENCES

1 Goodwin F. and Jamison K. Manic-depressive illness. Oxford University Press: New York, 1990

2 Mitchell P., Malhi G., Redwood B., Ball J. Bipolar disorder: treatment guide for consumers and carers. Australian and New Zealand College of Psychiatrists, 2003

3 Coryell W. The recognition and management of mania. Medscape Primary Care 2004; 6 (2): 1–4

4-7 Mitchell P., Malhi G., Redwood B., Ball J. Bipolar disorder: treatment guide for consumers and carers. Australian and New Zealand College of Psychiatrists, 2003

8 Parry B. and Haynes P. Mood disorders and the reproductive cycle. Journal of Gender-Specific Medicine 2003; (5): 53–58

9 Jamison K. An unquiet mind. Alfred A Knoff: New York, 1995

10 Jamison K. Stigma of manic depression: a psychologist's experience. Lancet 1998; 352 (9133): 1053

11–12 Ghaemi S., Ko J., Goodwin F. 'Cade's disease' and beyond: misdiagnosis, antidepressant use, and a proposed definition for bipolar spectrum disorder. Canadian Journal of Psychiatry 2002; 47:125–134

13 Goodwin F. cited in Sherman J. Misdiagnosis: manic-depression mistaken for schizophrenia. Schizophrenia Newsletter 1997

14 Goodwin F. and Jamison K. Manic-depressive illness. Oxford University Press: New York, 1990

15 McGuffin P. and Southwick L. Fifty years of the double helix and its impact on psychiatry. Australian and New Zealand Journal of Psychiatry 2003; 37 (6): 657–661

16 Goodwin F. and Jamison K. Manic-depressive illness. Oxford University Press: New York, 1990

17 Zaretsky A. Targeted psychosocial interventions for bipolar disorder. Bipolar Disorders 2003; 5 (2): 80–87

18–20 Goodwin F. and Jamison K. Manic-depressive illness. Oxford University Press: New York, 1990

21–22 Schou M. Forty years of lithium treatment. Archives of General Psychiatry 1997; 54 (1): 9–13

23–25 Goodwin F. and Jamison K. Manic-depressive illness. Oxford University Press: New York, 1990

26 Mitchell P., Malhi G., Redwood B., Ball J. Bipolar disorder: treatment guide for consumers and carers. Australian and New Zealand College of Psychiatrists, 2003

27 Goodwin F. and Jamison K. Manic-depressive illness. Oxford University Press: New York, 1990

28 Sachs G. and Rush A. Response, remission, and recovery in bipolar disorders: what are the realistic treatment goals? Journal of Clinical Psychiatry 2003; 64 (6): 18–22

29–31 Goodwin F. and Jamison K. Manic-depressive illness. Oxford University Press: New York, 1990

32 Zaretsky A. Targeted psychosocial interventions for bipolar disorder. Bipolar Disorders 2003; 5 (2): 80–87

33 Perry A., Tarrier N., Morriss R., McCarthy E., Limb K. Randomised controlled trial of efficacy of teaching patients with bipolar disorder to identify early symptoms of relapse and obtain treatment. British Medical Journal 1999; 318: 149–153

34 Geddes J. Prodromal symptoms may be identified by people with bipolar or unipolar depression. Evidence Based Mental Health 2003; 6 (4): 105

35 Sachs G and Rush A. Response, remission, and recovery in bipolar disorders: what are the realistic treatment goals? Journal of Clinical Psychiatry 2003; 64 (6): 18–22

36 Packer S. Family planning for women with bipolar disorder. Hospital and Community Psychiatry 1992; 43 (5): 479–82

37–38 Goodwin F. and Jamison K. Manic-depressive illness. Oxford University Press: New York, 1990

39 Batki S. Drug abuse, psychiatric disorders, and AIDS: dual and triple diagnosis. Western Journal of Medicine 1990; 152 (5): 547–52

40 Mitchell P., Malhi G., Redwood B., Ball J. Bipolar disorder: treatment guide for consumers and carers. Australian and New Zealand College of Psychiatrists, 2003

41 Jamison K. Stigma of manic depression: a psychologist's experience. Lancet 1998; 352 (9133): 1053

42–43 Stromwall L. Is social work's door open to people recovering from psychiatric disabilities? Social Work 2002; 47 (1): 75–83

44 Access Economics. Bipolar disorder: costs – an analysis of the burden of bipolar disorder and related suicide in Australia. SANE Australia, 2003